Lernkrimi Englisch

Deadly Business

Gina Billy
Joseph Sykes

compact

Weitere Informationen zu Compact Lernkrimis finden Sie am Ende des Buches und unter www.lernkrimi.de.

Baierbrunner Straße 27, 81379 München
Ausgabe 2016
4. Auflage

Redaktion: Helga Aichele, Gesa Füßle
Fachkorrektur: Nathalie Russell
Produktion: Ute Hausleiter
Titelillustration: Karl Knospe
Lernkrimi-Logo: Carsten Abelbeck
Gestaltung: EKH Werbeagentur GbR, textum GmbH
Umschlaggestaltung: EKH Werbeagentur GbR, Hartmut Baier

ISBN 978-3-8174-9215-2
381749215/4

www.compactverlag.de, www.lernkrimi.de, www.facebook.com/lernkrimi

Vorwort

Liebe Leserin, lieber Leser,
sicher zum Lernerfolg – mit Spaß und Spannung! Die Compact Lernkrimis mit ihrer Kombination aus Lektüre und didaktischem Übungsanteil eignen sich hervorragend, um breite Sprachkompetenzen in der Fremdsprache zu erwerben. Der Lerner wird dabei durch die spannende Handlung, das angemessene Sprachniveau und den stetig ansteigenden Schwierigkeitsgrad der Übungen gefördert und motiviert.
Entwickelt nach neuesten Erkenntnissen der Fremdsprachendidaktik, sind Compact Lernkrimis das ideale Medium für einen Lernerfolg im Selbststudium. Durch die kleinen Texteinheiten und den hohen Übungsanteil sind sie aber auch als Unterrichtslektüre bestens geeignet.

So lernen Sie mit Compact Lernkrimis:

- **Mit Begeisterung lernen:** Die packende Krimihandlung motiviert Sie beim Lesen des englischen Originaltextes.
- **Wissen intensivieren und erweitern:** Durch die Kombination aus didaktisierter Lektüre und textbezogenen Übungen testen und trainieren Sie Ihre Sprachkenntnisse effektiv. Vokabelangaben auf jeder Seite unterstützen Sie beim Lesen.
- **Systematisch lernen:** Knüpfen Sie an Ihr individuelles Sprachniveau an und setzen Sie eigene Lernziele – linear im Schwierigkeitsgrad ansteigend oder mit punktuellen Schwerpunkten von Grundwortschatz bis Hörverstehen.
- **Unabhängig sein:** Lernen Sie ganz individuell – wo und wann Sie wollen.

Viel Spaß beim **spannend Englisch lernen**
wünscht Ihnen

Prof. Dr. Christiane Neveling
Didaktik der romanischen Sprachen, Universität Leipzig

Inhalt

Deadly Business

Nach einer Idee von
Rebecca Jarosz

Joseph Sykes

1 Blackmail

How wonderfully cool the window feels against his face. But the moment of relaxation passes quickly. He feels stressed as he looks around his large, minimalist office. **Usually**, he enjoys the atmosphere of power his office gives him. But today he feels only **pressure** and even, he realizes, a **rising** panic.

He is a **successful** businessman who has worked extremely hard to get where he is now. God knows it hasn't been easy. And now there are these **threats**. Another letter arrived in the post this morning. He recognized the envelope as soon as he saw it. The letter said the same thing as the others before: They want his money. A lot of money. Just like that. And if he didn't pay...

Suddenly, there is a knock at the door.

"Come in?" he says. It isn't an **order**, but a question.

blackmail	Erpressung
usually	normalerweise, gewöhnlich
pressure	Druck
rising	(an)steigend
successful	erfolgreich
threat	Drohung
order	Befehl
to appear	sich zeigen, auftauchen
to breathe a sigh of relief	erleichtert aufatmen

The door seems to open slowly. He looks at his watch. Whoever could it be at this hour? he asks himself. My first meeting isn't until 9 o'clock.

A face **appears**. Janet, his secretary, smiles.

"Good morning, Mr Battlebolt," she says. "Did you and Mrs Battlebolt have an enjoyable evening last night?"

Richard Battlebolt **breathes a sigh of relief**. Of course! he thinks. It's Janet. Just Janet. He gives a small laugh.

Janet looks at him, a little **confused**. "I'll take that as a yes."

"What?" he asks. "Oh! Sorry, yes, our evening. Yes, it was lovely, thank you, Janet. We went to Lesley's favourite restaurant in Knightsbridge. Wonderful place. They really know how to cook..."

He stops, **mid-sentence**. A small man with short grey hair and a large, **pointed** chin has appeared beside Janet. He is holding a hat in his hands and is looking around the office.

"Sorry," Battlebolt says. "Erm... yes, they really know how to cook steak there..."

Battlebolt is speechless now as the small man steps right into his office and starts walking around the modernist sculpture by his bookcase. **What on earth** is he doing? Who *is* this man?

Janet notices her boss's confusion is slowly turning to **anger**.

"Mr Battlebolt," she says. "This is Charles Steede. Mr Steede said you wanted to see him. I told him he would need an **appointment**, but he said it was **urgent**."

confused	verwirrt
mid-sentence	mitten im Satz
pointed	spitz
What on earth...!	Was zum Teufel...!
anger	Zorn
appointment	Termin
urgent	dringend
to nod	nicken
to examine	untersuchen
moustache	Schnurrbart

Suddenly, everything makes sense. Charles Steede! Of course!

"Ah, yes, Mr Steede!" A nervous smile appears on Battlebolt's face. "Thank you for showing Mr Steede to my office, Janet." He **nods** at his secretary to make it clear that she should leave.

"Please, Mr Steede. Do take a seat."

But Steede has already hung up his jacket and pulled out the chair to sit down.

Battlebolt **examines** the man in front of him. He seems even smaller in the large chair. His grey **moustache** makes him look older than he probably is, Battlebolt thinks. In any case, Battlebolt had a very different picture of Mr Steede in his head. He thought Steede would look a bit like himself. Tall, maybe, and smartly dressed. Above all, he thought Mr Steede would look wealthy. But the little man sitting in front of him now looks more like an aging maths teacher than a private detective.

Exercise 1: Opposites. **Verbinden Sie die Gegenteile!**

1.	☐	tall	a)	poor
2.	☐	wealthy	b)	relaxed
3.	☐	easy	c)	short
4.	☐	stressed	d)	difficult

"As you know, I'm from Steede and Nug. You spoke to my partner, Mr Nug, yesterday, and told him you needed our help as soon as possible. So here I am. What can I do for you?"
Steede is looking Battlebolt straight in the eye, and Battlebolt simply looks back.
"What exactly is your problem, Mr Battlebolt?" Steede adds.
Battlebolt is a little shocked. People never speak to him so directly. He's the boss, the one with the authority and power. He gives orders. He doesn't receive them.
"Well then, if you don't want to talk to me, please excuse me, Mr Battlebolt," Steede stands up. "I certainly don't have time to waste..."
"I got another one this morning," Battlebolt says.
Steede smiles and sits back down. "Have you got it here?"
"Yes," Battlebolt says. "Just give me a moment."

The note is with the others, in a large envelope in the bottom drawer of his desk. He takes it out and passes it to Steede.
Steede takes out five smaller envelopes. Each one is the same. Battlebolt's business address is printed on the front in capital letters: CHIEF EXECUTIVE OFFICER, PISCES HEALTH, 1 UPPER BEAUMONT ROAD, LONDON. Steede's eyes move to the top right-hand corner, where he sees the Queen's head against a golden background. The letters were all sent first class (i).
Printed above the stamp it reads SOUTH ISLINGTON POST OFFICE. So the letters were all posted locally, he thinks.
Battlebolt reaches over and pushes one of the envelopes towards Steede.
"I received this one today."
Steede pulls out a sheet of white A4 paper with a short paragraph of text printed at the top. He looks up at Battlebolt. He's nervous in his own office, Steede thinks.
"So, let me see. 'Mr Battlebolt. I still haven't got my money. Maybe you think this is a joke? Well, imagine this. The front page of every newspaper in London announces: BUSINESSMAN BATTLEBOLT BRIBES ISLINGTON PLANNING OFFICER. Are you laughing now, Battlebolt? I don't think the people of Islington will want you as their MP when they know about your

in any case	wie dem auch sei
smartly dressed	elegant gekleidet
wealthy	vermögend
aging	alternd
to waste	verschwenden
chief executive officer (CEO)	Geschäftsführer
to imagine sth.	sich etw. vorstellen
to bribe	bestechen
planning officer	Beamter für Stadtplanung
MP (Member of Parliament)	Abgeordneter

Briefe, die am nächsten Tag ankommen sollen, werden in der Regel **first class** verschickt, d.h. mit einem Aufpreis. Die regulären Briefmarken sind **second class stamps.**

dirty business! Pay me £500,000 or officially stand down from election. You've got until Sunday. After that...'"

Steede reads the last sentence in silence and then turns to Battlebolt.

"I'm afraid I can't help you, Mr Battlebolt. You need a good lawyer and a lot of luck. Have you thought about going to the police?"

"The police?! Of course not! They don't understand the world of business. They don't understand how hard I've worked for Pisces Health. Not everybody has always liked me, but I've been successful. Does that make me a criminal, Mr Steede?"

"So..." Steede begins, but Battlebolt is still speaking.

"And it's quite clear who sent these letters," he says. "It's Maximilian Roth, CEO of Thornpharm. He knows Pisces Health is growing fast and he's scared. We're winning contracts with hospitals across the country. We can produce drugs at much lower costs than Thornpharm. Maximilian is the captain of a sinking ship. He's trying to put us out of business to save his own."

to stand down from election	von einer Wahl zurücktreten
lawyer	Anwalt
contract	*hier*: Auftrag
to put sb. out of business	jmd. aus dem Markt drängen
to come to an agreement	sich einigen
production facilities *pl*	Herstellungsanlagen
to depend	von etw. abhängen

"And *did* you bribe the planning officer, Mr Battlebolt?"

"We... came to an agreement," Battlebolt chooses his words carefully. "Pisces Health needs new production facilities. The site in Islington is perfect. I just wanted to make sure..."

"Did you or didn't you bribe the planning officer? It's a simple question."

Battlebolt thinks carefully for a moment, then replies, "That depends if you're going to help me, Mr Steede."

Exercise 2: Prepositions. Lesen Sie weiter und ergänzen Sie die fehlenden Präpositionen!

along | on | out of | to | towards | with

Steede steps **1.** ___ 1 Upper Beaumont Road and starts walking back **2.** ___ the underground station. Islington is slowly coming **3.** ___ life. Office workers march **4.** ___ the street with their morning latte – breakfast **5.** ___ the go. Black cabs and red buses **compete** **6.** ___ builders to make the most noise.

Battlebolt has told him everything. He has it all: money, power, a beautiful wife and a young son, and political ambitions. Which means, of course, that he has everything to lose.

If the general public finds out about Battlebolt's dirty games, he'll never be elected. He'll lose his job, maybe even his wife. And the police will most certainly want to investigate his corrupt activities.

But who knows? Who's sending the ransom letters? Battlebolt is sure it's the CEO of Thornpharm, Maximilian Roth. It would make sense, Steede thinks, but...

Something isn't right. Battlebolt seemed too sure it was Max Roth.

to compete	*hier*: kämpfen
to lose	verlieren
to elect	wählen
to investigate	untersuchen, ermitteln

When Steede asked if anyone else might **bear a grudge** against him, he seemed shocked. No, Mr Steede! his face seemed to say. How could anyone hate me, Richard Battlebolt, CEO of a very successful pharmaceutical company?
But there's something even **stranger**, Steede thinks. Battlebolt and the planning officer did their deal alone in his office. So where was the **spy**? Hiding behind the single bookcase in his minimalist office? Spying through the window with a **pair of binoculars**?! Of course not. Every possible scenario seems absurd.
Steede crosses the road. A young girl is standing by the station entrance, **offering** free newspapers. "No, thank you," Steede says, when she tries to put one into his hand. Steede continues into the station and then stops. Who was the woman on the front page of that newspaper? he asks himself. I'm sure I recognize her face.

to bear a grudge	einen Groll hegen
strange	seltsam, merkwürdig
spy	Spion
pair of binoculars	Fernglas
to offer	anbieten
hospital ward	Krankenstation
to hurry	sich beeilen

Exercise 3: Match up the phrases. Verbinden Sie die Begriffe!

1. ☐ waste	a) a grudge
2. ☐ bear	b) an agreement
3. ☐ come to	c) a promise
4. ☐ make	d) time

He turns and walks back to the girl at the entrance and takes a newspaper from her.

ELECTION SPECIAL: CANDIDATE FARNHAM MAKES HOSPITAL JOBS PROMISES.

In the picture, Lindsay Farnham is standing in a **hospital ward** with two nurses to her left and a patient to her right. She has a big smile on her face, showing her large white teeth.

"Farnham," Steede says to himself. "Of course, Lindsay Farnham!"

Steede smiles, puts the newspaper under his arm and **hurries** into the station.

2 A False Identity

Ben Nug is on the phone to his new girlfriend when Steede arrives back at their relatively small office near Finsbury Park, in the north of Islington. The two have only been together for a few weeks, but Nug is totally **smitten**.

"Must go," he says when he hears Steede arrive. "But I'll ring you later, okay? Love you!... Can't wait to see you... I know, you too!... Lots of love." He ends the call by making a kissing noise and hopes Steede hasn't heard him.

"Hey, Charles!" He walks out into the **hallway**. "What's all this with Battlebolt? Why does a **fat cat** like him need our services?"

"Does Emma know you tell all your girlfriends you love them within the first month?" Steede asks, ignoring Nug's question.

Steede is almost 20 years older than his Indian partner, and he sees himself as a sort of father figure to him. They are **equal** partners in their work, but Steede has an extra 20 years' experience in unsuccessful relationships and bitterness. You mustn't make the same mistakes as me, he tells Nug time and time again.

"Her name is Emily," Nug replies and rolls his eyes. "And no, she... I'll tell you about her later. What does Battlebolt want?"

smitten	vernarrt
hallway	Flur
ϟ fat cat	Bonze
equal	*hier*: gleichwertig
to blackmail	erpressen
factory	Fabrik
permission	Zulassung
to suspect	verdächtigen
to lean	sich lehnen
doorframe	Türrahmen

Steede smiles and the two walk into his office.
"He's being **blackmailed**. Pisces Health needs a new **factory**. He wants it to be in Islington. But he knew it would be difficult to get **permission**. So he bribed the Islington Council planning officer. The problem is that someone found out and has started sending him blackmail letters. Battlebolt has to pay out £500,000 or step down from the election or his blackmailer will go to the press."
"*Oooh*, that's not very nice," Nug says sarcastically. "Any idea who it is?"
Steede tells his partner about Maximilian Roth.
"But I **suspect** someone else," he says. "Her."
He throws the newspaper at Nug.

Exercise 4: Missing words. Lesen Sie weiter und ergänzen Sie die fehlenden Begriffe!

body | door | eyes | thick | handsome | information

Steede's 1. ______ young partner **leans** against the 2. ______. Unlike Steede, Nug is very tall and well-built, and his large 3. ______ seems to fill the **door-frame**. He runs his right hand through his 4. ______ black hair, while his light grey 5. ______ quickly scan the front page of the newspaper for the key 6. ______.

"Lindsay Farnham. I see what you mean," he says after a few seconds. "She's quite radical, you know. They interviewed her on the radio a few days ago. 'Power to the people', 'Bring down the bankers', and all that. Politically, she's Battlebolt's exact **opposite**."

"I know, and have you read this part here?" Steede asks, pointing to a paragraph halfway down the front page. "'There is no **doubt**. Richard Battlebolt has **donated** money to our hospital for one reason alone: he wants to buy the people of Islington's votes. A vote for Battlebolt is a vote for the fat cats.'"

"Roth or Farnham, Farnham or Roth," Nug says and pulls a couple of dead leaves off the dried-up plant in the corner of the room. "Which shall we start with?"

Steede smiles. "One for you and one for me."

opposite	Gegenteil
doubt	Zweifel
to donate	spenden
to sigh	seufzen
to pretend	tun als ob
to change the subject	das Thema wechseln
golden opportunity	einmalige Gelegenheit
to set the record straight	eine Sache richtigstellen
briefcase	Aktentasche/ -koffer

The receptionist takes a deep breath and **sighs**.

"I'm afraid it's quite complicated, Mr... Mr...?"

"Patel," Ben Nug answers.

"...Mr Patel. Yes, Mr Roth is a very busy man. You need to fill in a few documents first. Give me your email address and I'll send you them now. Oh, and I need a copy of your press card. I'll take a copy of that now."

"Certainly," Nug says, "but I'll need a PCCN."

"A what?" the receptionist asks. "I don't think I..."

"A PCCN?!" Nug **pretends** to be surprised. "A press card copy notice. You know what that is, right?"

Of course, the truth is that 'press card copy notices' don't even exist. It's the same every time. Nug creates a false identity – Mr Patel – and says he needs a 'PCCN'. And the receptionists never question him. The truth is, they feel stupid. Of course, they haven't heard of the press card copy notification! But they're afraid to ask what it is. They just nod and smile and say...

Exercise 5: Word spiral. Ergänzen Sie die Wortspirale!

1	2	3	4	5	6
20	21	22	23	24	7
19	32	33	34	25	8
18	31	36	35	26	9
17	30	29	28	27	10
16	15	14	13	12	11

1-4: the CEO of Thornpharm
4-7: At the end of your arm is your...
7-10: In the middle of the ocean, the water is very...
10-14: a living thing with leaves and sometimes flowers
14-18: facts, not fiction
18-23: the state of the body
23-27: They decided to stay in an expensive 5-star...
27-31: big
31-36: messages sent via the Internet

"I'm sorry, Mr Patel, I don't think we have any... erm..."
"Really? How strange. Anyway," Nug says, to **change the subject**, "it's a shame I can't see him today. I can't come back tomorrow or Friday, and it'll be too late by Monday. Mr Roth is missing a **golden opportunity** to **set the record straight**."
He pulls his bright blue scarf round his neck and picks up his **brief-case**. He turns and looks around the huge lobby. There are lots of plants and pieces of artwork. The whole place feels more like a hotel

than an office building. A large **sign** is hanging on the back wall: 'Thornpharm: Your health in good hands.'
"Wait a minute, Mr Patel. What exactly do you mean by 'set the record straight'? I'm not sure I follow you."
Nug turns around again and puts his briefcase back on the floor.
"Yesterday I interviewed Richard Battlebolt, CEO of..."
"Yes, yes, I know who Battlebolt is," the receptionist replies.
"Okay, well, in the interview he talked a lot about his company's successes in the past few months and his plans for the future. And he **compared** Pisces Health to Thornpharm. The statistics were quite shocking. He didn't paint a positive picture of your company at all. Usually I would **give** you much more **notice**, of course, but I thought..."
"What are you trying to say, Mr Patel?"
"I'm trying to say that I'm offering Mr Roth a chance. A chance to stop Thornpharm from looking like shi..." Nug puts his hand over his mouth and pretends to stop himself. "Sorry, erm, a chance to stop the company from looking *quite bad* in the press."
The receptionist doesn't respond. She just picks up the phone and dials a number.
"Paul?... Hi, it's Sheena. Do you know what Mr Roth's **schedule** looks like today?... Oh, okay. Thanks. There's a journalist from *Pharmaceutical Weekly* here at reception. He'd like to see Mr Roth. I think Mr Roth will probably want to see him, too."
Two minutes later, Nug is sitting on a very large but uncomfortable chair in Maximilian Roth's office.
"I think the word Mr Battlebolt used was 'future-proof'," Nug is saying to Maximilian Roth. "Yes, that was it. He said Pisces

sign	*hier*: Schild
to compare	vergleichen
to give sb. notice	jmd. vorwarnen
schedule	Zeitplan
decade	Jahrzehnt
to frown	die Stirn runzeln
to interrupt	unterbrechen
voice	Stimme

Health will still be around in future **decades** because it's 'future-proof'."
Max Roth leans forward over his large desk and **frowns**. He writes a few words on a piece of paper and then looks Nug straight in the eye.
"Let me say one thing," he says. Silence.
"You can say much more than..." Nug begins, but Roth continues.
"Richard Battlebolt has no idea what he is talking about." Silence again.
"Oh... I didn't quite expect you to say that, Mr Roth."
"Battlebolt is small fish. Yes, Pisces is growing. But Battlebolt can't compete at global level. Pisces won't be around forever." Roth laughs. "I know that for sure. In fact..."

Exercise 6: Unscramble the text. Lesen Sie weiter und bringen Sie die Textabschnitte in die richtige Reihenfolge!

a) Nug cannot believe it. The police! He looks at Roth. Roth's face has gone white.

b) A knock on the door **interrupts** Roth. He gives Nug a false, professional smile.

c) "Good morning, Mr Roth," says a man's **voice**. "I'm Sergeant Armstead. This is Sergeant Piers. Sorry to interrupt your meeting, but it's urgent."

d) "Please excuse me one moment, Mr Patel. Come in!"

1	2	3	4

"Mr Patel?" Sergeant Armstead asks. Nug turns and nods.
"Yes, that's me."
"The receptionist told us you were in the middle of an interview. But I'm sorry, I'll have to ask you to leave. I hope you're able to finish your article another..."

to disappear	verschwinden
guilty	schuldig
to accompany	begleiten
law	Gesetz

...*time*? Nug thinks.
"...with someone else, I mean."
Nug tries to hide his surprise, but his heart is pumping adrenaline around his body. What are the police here for? The blackmailing? Another crime? He turns back to Roth. The look of power and authority has **disappeared** from his face. He looks scared, Nug thinks. He looks **guilty**.
"Mr Patel?"
"Yes, of course, Sergeant. I'll just pack my things away. Thank you for your time, Mr Roth. I'm sure I can write some very positive things about Thornpharm." But his words are empty, meaningless and, he thinks, stupid.
But Roth doesn't notice. "Yes," he says without looking at Nug. "I'm sure you can."
Nug walks out of the room and down the corridor. Paul, the young man who **accompanied** him to Roth's office, is already waiting for him.
"Come with me, Mr Patel. It's this way down to reception."
"Could I just use the bathroom, please?"
He doesn't wait for Paul's reply. He pushes open the door to the men's toilets and takes out his mobile phone.
"Charles?... Yes, I got the interview. But listen, we were interrupted. By the police... Yes, I know. Roth looked guilty as hell. Listen, Roth is in trouble with the **law**. There's no doubt about it. I'm not going anywhere. Not until I know what's going on."

Exercise 7: Word forms. Ergänzen Sie das jeweilige Substantiv oder Adjektiv!

Noun	Adjective
1. mobility	______________
2. ______________	powerful
3. guilt	______________
4. ______________	surprised

3 Information and Technology

The information board at Islington Community College is much bigger than Charles Steede imagined. His eyes scan the board: Arabic... Art and design... Astrology.... He is surprised to see how many different courses are on offer. He jumps to History... Indian cuisine... and then he finds it: Information Technology.

There seem to be a number of IT classes, but Steede finds the one he is looking for immediately: Wednesday, 12:00–1:00, IT for beginners. Room 2.13. Course leader: LF. Steede looks at his watch[i]. Five past one. He heads to the lift and presses '2'. Maybe she's still in the classroom.

When the lift doors open onto the second floor, Steede hurries out and walks straight into a pretty young woman with long brown hair. "Sorry!" the young woman says with a smile, and shows her large white teeth. It is a typically British reaction to apologize even though Steede walked into her, and not the other way round.

"No, *I'm* sorry," Steede says and returns the smile. "I wasn't looking where I was going." As he speaks, he realizes whom he is speaking to. "Is it... Mrs Farnham?" he asks.

"*Miss* Farnham," she corrects him. "But yes, that's me."

"Great!" he says. "You're just the person I was looking for."

The lift doors have closed now, and Steede thinks he sees annoyance

> Beachten Sie die verschiedenen Übersetzungen für „Uhr": Eine Armbanduhr wird immer als **watch** bezeichnet, alle anderen Uhren heißen **clock.** Standuhren nennt man **grandfather clock.**

in Lindsay Farnham's face. She's missed her opportunity to escape and now she has to talk to him.
"How can I help you?" she asks. The smile is back.

Exercise 8: Where do you learn that? Verbinden Sie die Kurse mit dem Raum, in dem man sie lernt!

1. ☐ Indian cuisine	a) studio
2. ☐ IT	b) kitchen
3. ☐ art and design	c) computer room
4. ☐ gymnastics	d) gymnasium

"I'm interested in learning about Internet security," Steede says.
"The class is on a Monday evening," Farnham answers, and takes a notepad and pen out of her handbag. "But we're halfway through this course at the moment."

"Maybe you can tell me a thing or two now," Steede says.
"Erm… I'm actually on a break. I only have five minutes," Farnham replies, as she writes down a few words in the notepad. "But the new course begins next month. Here, this is the course code. You'll need that when you register." She tears out a slip of paper and gives it to him.

information technology	Informationstechnik
annoyance	Verärgerung
to escape	entkommen
actually	in der Tat, eigentlich
to register	sich anmelden
to tear out	ausreißen

"Thank you. Does the course cover computer hacking?"

"Well, yes... You'll learn about security in general. And that includes staying safe from Internet hacking, yes."
"Because I thought you might be an expert on hacking, Miss Farnham. I imagine your knowledge of IT is very useful for your political career. I mean, I'm sure it must be very useful to know all your opponents' scandalous secrets, right? I know I'd **be tempted** to find them out if I knew how?"
Lindsay Farnham's smile has disappeared now, and she is looking at Steede **suspiciously**. Steede stares back for a second or two, then smiles.
"I'm joking, Miss Farnham!" he laughs. "Of course I don't really think you're a **crooked** politician. You haven't been elected yet!"
Farnham gives an uncertain smile and raises her eyebrows.
"I've just remembered. I think the course is already full. Excuse me." She pushes her long hair from her shoulders and walks quickly to the stairs at the end of the corridor. Steede watches her disappear from view and then heads in the other direction. Most of the classrooms are dark and empty, and the corridor is quiet. Only one classroom is lit up. Steede looks through the window to see a man, standing, typing a text message into his mobile phone. 2.12 reads the number on the door.

to be tempted	versucht sein
suspiciously	misstrauisch
ϟ crooked	unehrlich
to grant	erteilen, gewähren
to be in the mood for sth.	Lust haben auf etw.
bun	*hier*: Dutt

He walks to the next room along, 2.13, and tries the door. Locked, of course. In the dark room, the screen of a laptop is shining brightly on a desk at the front. A web page is open to show a man's face smiling next to the text. The face looks familiar. Steede tries to read the headline from where he is standing at the window. 'Shock decision: Permission for new drugs factory **granted**.' His eyes move back to the face in the photograph. It looks young, happy and carefree in the photo. That's why Steede didn't recognize him. But there's no doubt about it. It's Richard Battlebolt.

"We could go to that new tapas bar next to the cinema," Ben Nug suggests. "Or are you **in the mood for** a curry?"
A group of businessmen leave the Thornpharm headquarters, and Nug watches them cross the road. But still no police officers have left the building. He quickly looks at his mobile phone to check the time – 1:16 – and then puts it back to his ear.
"Yes... No, I don't think it's too expensive, Emily. One of my mates went last week. He said it was really nice... Yeah?... Okay, I'll pick you up at 8... Yeah, okay... Love you... bye!"
He ends the call and puts his phone in his jacket pocket, then takes it straight back out and looks at the time again. 1:16. Of course, he thinks, and laughs at himself. "I must be growing old."
"Or going mad," says a woman's voice to his right. He turns and sees the Thornpharm receptionist. "Start talking to yourself and soon the men in white coats will come for you!"
Nug laughs. "I didn't know anyone was there."

Exercise 9: Unscramble the words. Lesen Sie weiter und bringen Sie die Buchstaben in die richtige Reihenfolge!

The receptionist takes out a cigarette and **1.** gthils ____________ it. She has a young face – in her late 20s, Nug guesses. She has her **2.** krad ____________ hair tied up in a tight **bun**, and she is wearing a short, black **3.** strik ____________.

"Don't worry. I wasn't **4.** gypsin ______________ on you," she says. "Although I'm a little **5.** udprrisse ______________ to find you here in my private **6.** gnomiks ______________ area. I thought you left half an hour ago."

Nug laughs again. "I'm a journalist, remember? I'm waiting here in the **shadows** for the police to come out with Mr Roth. Then I can take photos of him and cause a scandal."
The receptionist stares with a look of shock on her face.
"I'm joking! I work for *Pharmaceutical Weekly*, not a **gossip mag**. My colleague is picking me up. But he's late. Very late."
"Oh!" the receptionist says with a laugh. "I thought..."
"No, no... I was just trying to be funny. Unsuccessfully," he says **flirtatiously**, pretending to look ashamed. But once again the receptionist **is fooled**, just as she was by the 'PCCN'. She laughs again and blows smoke from her mouth.

shadow	Schatten
ϟ gossip mag	Klatsch-magazin
flirtatiously	kokett
to be fooled	hereingelegt, getäuscht
to take a drag	einen Zug nehmen

"No, I think you should forget a career in comedy, Mr Patel," she says.
"Call me Josh." He remembers her name straight away, but adds a pause for effect. "Was it... Sheena?"
"That's right." Sheena smiles and **takes a drag** of her cigarette.
"I hope Mr Roth is okay. I mean, I hope the police didn't come with bad news."

Sheena **hesitates**, then looks up and makes eye contact with Nug. "I probably shouldn't tell you this, but... it's about his father. His parents live in Monaco. They have lived there for years. But last month, his father went missing. Mr Roth went out to Monaco to support his mother straight away. He only got back yesterday. And the police are here because..." Sheena looks from side to side to check they are alone. "We don't know for sure, but my colleagues think his father is dead."

"That's terrible," Nug says. Now the **sympathy** in his voice is real. "Poor Mr Roth. Thanks for letting me know, Sheena. I know to leave him in peace, now."

to hesitate	zögern
sympathy	Mitgefühl
skyscraper	Wolkenkratzer
to loosen	lockern
to tense	anspannen, sich verspannen
to whisper	flüstern

Richard Battlebolt closes the door to his office and sighs. He walks over to the window and looks out onto the **skyscrapers** of the city, then down to the ground far below. He **loosens** his tie. The stress is making him feel sick now. His mobile phone rings and his muscles **tense**.

"Go away," he **whispers**. "Go away, go away, go away."

He counts to seven, his lucky number, then takes his mobile phone out of his jacket pocket.

He sees the name 'Lesley' on the screen.

"Go away," he says, one last time, then accepts the call.

"Hello, darling. Are you all right?"

"Richard, there's no petrol in the Jaguar!"

"Oh, darling, I'm sorry. I forgot," he replies.

"I'm already late!" Lesley continues. "I'm meeting Gillian and Victoria at 1:30. How am I going to get there without any petrol in the car? I specifically asked you to fill it up, didn't I?"

Battlebolt **feels his blood boil**. She has no idea! he thinks. All that matters to her is shopping and socializing. She **doesn't have a** damn **clue**!

"Listen, Lesley. I'm extremely busy. I'm sorry about the car, but I can't speak right now. I'll ring you later this afternoon, okay?"

He thinks about the words in the blackmail letters.

'You might feel powerless and **trapped** now, Battlebolt, but wait until this scandal brings you down. This is nothing compared with how you will feel then.'

Battlebolt closes his eyes and puts his head in his left hand.

to feel one's blood boil	kochen vor Wut
to not have a clue	keine Ahnung haben
trapped	gefangen
to snap at sb.	jmd. anblaffen, anschnauzen
condition	Bedingung

Exercise 10: Question and answer. Beantworten Sie die Fragen!

1. What can Mr Battlebolt see outside his office?

___

2. Why does Mr Battlebolt feel sick?

___

3. Why is Mrs Battlebolt angry with her husband?

___

4. How does Mr Battlebolt end the call with his wife?

___

"Richard? Are you listening to me? Richard?"
"Just leave it, Lesley!" he **snaps**. "Just leave it!"
'Pay £500,000 or officially stand down.' Those were the **conditions**. It's impossible. There's no way out. The blackmailer is right. He's trapped.
"Richard! What's wrong with you? I can't believe..."
Battlebolt ends the call by throwing the phone across his desk. He can still hear the final words of the very first letter in his head.
'You think you're a high-flyer, Battlebolt. And you're right. But don't forget: the higher you fly, the further[i] you have to fall.'
Then Richard Battlebolt looks out of the window again. It's a long way down.

Die Steigerung von **far** ist **farther** oder **further.** Ursprünglich ist die Bedeutung von **farther** wörtlich, also „weiter weg", während **further** eine übertragene Bedeutung hat (**for further information** ... – für weitere Informationen ...). Heutzutage wird further jedoch sehr viel häufiger verwendet als farther.

4 Battlebolt's Blood

The coffee shop opposite Islington Community College is quiet, which is perfect for Steede and Nug. An old man is reading the newspaper in the corner at the back, and a young couple are talking over cups of hot chocolate near the **counter**. Steede and Nug are the only other customers.

Nug carries two coffees to the high stools by the window, where his partner is sitting.

"Thanks," Steede says. He keeps his eyes on the entrance to the college across the road.

"You're welcome. Any sign of Lindsay Farnham?"

"Not yet. It's only 2:55. According to the information board, her last class finishes at three. So she should leave in the next ten minutes or so. Hopefully."

Nug **takes a sip** of his coffee. "So, what exactly did you find out about her?"

"As I said on the phone, nothing concrete. But she didn't like it when I said the word 'hacking'. I think I touched a nerve. Then, when I looked through her classroom window, she had an article open on her laptop: 'Shock decision: Permission for new drugs factory granted', complete with photo of Battlebolt. She's **keeping**

counter	Tresen, Theke
to take a sip	einen Schluck nehmen
to keep an eye on sb./sth.	jmd./etw. im Auge behalten
convinced	überzeugt
to arrest sb.	jmd. verhaften
rumour	Gerücht
awful	schrecklich
purpose	Zweck

an eye on Battlebolt because she's blackmailing him, I'm convinced of it, Ben. Anyway, tell me about Roth. Why are you sure it isn't him?"

Exercise 11: Verbs. Lesen Sie weiter und setzen Sie die korrekte Verbfom ein! Verwenden Sie, wenn möglich, die Kurzform!

"The receptionist 1. tell ________ me he's been in Monaco for the past month. His father 2. go ________ missing there. So the police 3. not be ________ at his office to arrest him for blackmail. They were there to tell him... well, I 4. not know ________. But 5. there be ________ a rumour that his father is dead. But anyway, whether his father is dead or not, we can rule out Roth."

"God, how awful. Who would have thought?"
Steede is about to take another sip of coffee, when two young women walk out of the college.
"That's her, Ben! The one in the red coat with the brown hair."
Nug quickly stands up, pulls on his coat, takes one last sip of coffee, then he is out of the door and heading down the street. The two women are walking quite quickly. Walking with a purpose, Nug thinks. They have somewhere to be.
After about 100 metres, the women turn right up a side street.

Nug hasn't crossed the road to their side yet, and he's worried he's going to lose them. There isn't a **break** in the **traffic**, and none of the drivers are stopping to let him cross. The women are walking further and further up the street. He looks to the right. A double-decker bus is slowing down, and for a moment, Nug thinks it is slowing to let him cross. But instead, the bus slows to a halt right in front of him, stopping for a group of passengers. His view of the side street is now completely blocked.

"Shit!" Nug hurries to the front of the bus to get a clear view. But it's too late. The women have disappeared.

Three more cars pass, and finally, there is a break. Nug runs across the road to the sound of **car horns** from angry drivers. He raises his hand to say sorry, but doesn't look back. He continues up the side street, but the women are nowhere to be seen.

break	*hier*: Lücke
traffic	Verkehr
car horn	Autohupe
to blink	blinzeln
ϟ liquid lunch	Alkohol statt Mittagessen
change	Wechselgeld

"For God's sake! Where have they gone?" Nug says out loud, then realizes he is talking to himself again and laughs quietly to himself. Maybe Sheena the receptionist was right, he thinks. Maybe I am going mad.

He looks up the street and sees nothing but houses and parked cars. There are no shops or cafés. There are no...

Nug **blinks**. Then he blinks again. Yes, there is something. A little further up the street, he sees a sign above a black door: 'Jazz Bar'. It appeared from nowhere! Nug laughs again. "I'm definitely going mad."

The discreet little bar is much busier inside than Nug expected. A few city workers in suits are enjoying a late **liquid lunch**, but most of the people in the bar are younger, probably students. *Don't worry*

about a thing, Bob Marley sings to them from the loud speakers. *'Cause every little thing gonna be alright.*
The two women are standing at the bar. Lindsay Farnham has taken off her red coat and hung it on the back of a chair at a table near the bar. Nug decides to sit on a stool at the end of the bar, just behind Farnham's chair.
"Thank you," Farnham says to the barman and takes her **change**.
"Cheers, Linds," her friend says and raises her glass. "Orange juice today, champagne next week, when you're an MP."
"I don't want to count my chickens before they're hatched, Maria," Farnham tells her friend, and the pair take their drinks over to their table and sit down. "I haven't been elected yet. Battlebolt might still win. It's neck and neck."

Exercise 12: Idioms. Finden Sie im Text die englischen Entsprechungen zu den deutschen idiomatischen Ausdrücken.

1. Es ist ein Kopf-an-Kopf-Rennen.

____

2. Er behält sie gerade im Auge.

____

3. Ich glaube, ich habe einen wunden Punkt berührt.

____

4. Man soll den Tag nicht vor dem Abend loben!

____

"Battlebolt?" Maria pulls a **disgusted** face. "That snake? He won't win. I promise you, I know he won't win."

"You can't be sure of that."

Nug has ordered a drink and is pretending to read a newspaper now. But really he is keeping a close eye on Lindsay Farnham and her friend, Maria.

"And..." Farnham adds. "Oh, I don't know."

"What is it?" Maria asks. "You can tell me, Linds."

Farnham sighs. "Maybe I'm being paranoid. But..." she lowers her voice to a whisper, and Nug has to concentrate hard to hear each word. "I sometimes feel that Battlebolt is spying on me."

"Spying on you?" Maria looks shocked, and pushes her short, dark brown hair behind her ear.

"A man stopped me in the corridor earlier today and asked me a few questions about the internet security course. He seemed normal at first, but then he wanted to know whether I was a computer hacker."

"What?!"

"I know, strange, right? Shortly afterwards, I saw him looking through the window into my classroom. He stood there for about a minute, staring into the room. **Perhaps** it meant nothing. But something tells me he is **connected** to Battlebolt. Maybe he's looking for information which he can use against me. Maybe he wants to create a public scandal. Something like that. What do you think, Maria?"

Maria turns towards the bar and Nug quickly looks down at the newspaper. He can feel her eyes burning into the side of his face. Was he listening a little *too* carefully?

disgusted	empört
perhaps	vielleicht
connected	verbunden
to not give a damn about sth.	auf etw. pfeifen
to hurt sb.	jmd. weh tun
attentively	aufmerksam
to trust	vertrauen
impatient	ungeduldig

No, Maria turns back to Lindsay. She takes another sip of her orange juice and then leans a little closer.
"To be honest, I don't know. Maybe Battlebolt is playing dirty, maybe he isn't. But it wouldn't surprise me. It's in his nature."
"In his nature?"
"Yes, he... How can I explain this? He **doesn't give a damn about** the consequences of his actions. He doesn't care if he **hurts** other people." Maria pauses and looks towards Nug once again.
This time, Nug's face is buried in the newspaper, but he's listening **attentively** to Maria's every word.
"His whole life is a lie."
"But... I... What are you talking about? What sort of a lie?"
"Listen, Lindsay. You mustn't tell anyone. Not many people know this. Only a couple of my best friends. I've been friends with you for a while and I know I can **trust** you, so..."
"What *is* it, Maria?" the young IT teacher is getting **impatient**.
"Richard Battlebolt is my father."

Exercise 13: True or false? Welche Aussagen sind korrekt? Markieren Sie mit richtig ✓ oder falsch – !

1. Farnham thinks her political rival is spying on her. ❒
2. Nug is pretending to read a book. ❒
3. Maria is drinking orange juice. ❒
4. Nobody else knows Maria's secret. ❒

Nug can't believe what he is hearing. This is golden! But he doesn't react. He just turns the page of the newspaper and takes a sip from his bottle of beer.

Lindsay Farnham can't believe it either. Her mouth has dropped wide open and she gives a nervous laugh in horror and **disbelief**.
"Your father?"
"Yes, my father. He had a one-night stand with my mum. And Mum was unlucky. She got **pregnant**. She told Battlebolt, but he didn't want anything to do with her. Or the baby. Me."
"But how did you... When did you...?"
"I found out he was my father a few years ago, while I was pregnant with Alfie. My mum saw his photograph in the paper. 'That's him,' she said. 'That's your father.' She lost contact with him when I was born. He **refused** to speak to her. And her family didn't support her either. She'd brought shame on them, her father said. So my mum was 20 years old and alone with a newborn baby. And she really was alone. Everyone said it was her own stupid **fault**. That she should have been more careful."

disbelief	Unglaube
pregnant	schwanger
to refuse	sich weigern
fault	Schuld
nursery	Kindergarten

"I can't believe it, Maria. Battlebolt. The bastard."
"Exactly. He left us, and now he's making millions. He's really rich! It makes me sick. I may have Battlebolt's blood in my veins, but I hate the man."
At that moment, Nug's phone begins to ring. Not now, Emily! he thinks, when he sees the name on the screen.
Maria turns and looks at him one last time, then looks at her watch.
"Listen, Linds. I don't have much time. I have to go and pick Alfie up from **nursery**. Do you want to walk down with me?"
"Sure. I'm heading that way anyway."
The two women finish their drinks and put their coats on.
"I'm going to take him to the park for a while," Maria opens the door. "Then I'm bringing him with me to my next class..."

Exercise 14: Translation. **Lesen Sie weiter und übersetzen Sie die deutschen Begriffe ins Englische!**

The door closes and they're gone. Nug wants to **1.** folgen ___________ them, but he can't. They've seen him, and Maria seems **2.** misstrauisch ___________ already.

"Ben!" comes a **3.** Stimme ___________ from his phone. "Are you listening to me?" She sounds **4.** ungeduldig ___________.

"Sorry, darling," he tells his girlfriend. "I think I have to work **5.** spät ___________."

5 Family Business

The large clock on the wall reads exactly seven o'clock when Charles Steede pushes open the large double doors and steps into the corridor. He looks at his own watch. 6:56. Good, he thinks. The clock's fast. I still have a few minutes.

Steede finds room 1.01, the photography studio at Islington Community College, at the far end of the corridor. A timetable on the door **confirms** he is in the right place: Wednesday, 5:00–7:00, The Art of Photography, Maria Johnson.

He places his briefcase on a table next to the door and takes out a small digital **voice recorder** and a packet of batteries. He changes the batteries as quickly as possible, then turns on the voice recorder and holds it about half a metre from his mouth.

"Testing, testing," he says quietly.

Testing, testing, the machine repeats back to him.

Steede puts the voice recorder in the front pocket of his suit and closes his briefcase. He **scratches** his long chin and straightens his hat, then stands back.

Thirty seconds later, the door to room 1.01 opens and the pupils – mostly middle-aged, middle-class women – start to leave.

to confirm	bestätigen
voice recorder	Aufzeichnungsgerät für Gespräche
to scratch sth.	etw. kratzen
exhausting	sehr anstrengend
felt-tip pen	Filzstift
to introduce sb.	jmd. vorstellen, bekanntmachen
curiosity	Neugier

"See you later, Alfie!" Steede hears one of them say. "Be a good boy for Mummy, won't you!"
"He's not always as good as he was tonight," Maria's voice replies. "Believe me, he can be **exhausting**."

Exercise 15: Homonyms. **Viele englische Wörter haben mehrere Bedeutungen und können unterschiedlich übersetzt werden. Kreuzen Sie die *falsche* Übersetzung an!**

1. watch	**a)** ☐ Hexe	**b)** ☐ anschauen	**c)** ☐ Uhr
2. suit	**a)** ☐ Anzug	**b)** ☐ süß	**c)** ☐ passen
3. place	**a)** ☐ Stück	**b)** ☐ Ort	**c)** ☐ hinstellen
4. pupil	**a)** ☐ Schüler	**b)** ☐ Pupille	**c)** ☐ Kanzel

When all of the pupils have left, Steede knocks on the door and steps into the classroom. Maria Johnson is packing her bag. Her young son is sitting on the floor and colouring in a picture of a giraffe with his **felt-tip pens**.
"Good evening," Steede says with a smile, and takes his hat off. "It's a little warmer in here. It's grown quite cold outside. Sorry, I should **introduce** myself. My name is Charles Steede. I'd like to ask for your help, Miss Johnson."
"Oh?" Maria replies with **curiosity** in her voice. "What can I do for you, Mr Steede?"
There are times when Steede must work slowly and carefully, when the trick is to be subtle. This isn't one of those times.
He remembers Nug's words to him. *Johnson told Farnham she knew Battlebolt wouldn't win the election. In fact, she promised her that he wouldn't win!*

"I want to know why you wrote these letters."
Steede opens his briefcase and drops two of the brown envelopes on the table.
Johnson's eyes open wide with shock. "I've... I've never seen them in my life!"
"This is my theory," Steede ignores Johnson's comment. "You've had a hard life. As a child, you lived alone with your mother. She didn't get any support from her family... or from your father."
Maria throws her bag over her shoulder and picks up her son's felt-tip pens. "Put your coat on, Alfie. There's a good boy."
"And now you're in the same situation as your mother." Steede takes out a newspaper article which he printed off the internet an hour earlier: TRAGIC CAR CRASH KILLS NEW GRANDMOTHER.
"Your boyfriend left you while you were pregnant. And your mother died shortly after your son was born. I imagine that things have been extremely hard for you."
Maria turns off the lights and pulls her son out into the corridor.
"No," she shouts back at Steede. "You can't imagine it."
"But I can see the effects. You can't **afford** a babysitter, so you bring your son to work with you in the evenings. That's really quite an extreme situation, Maria."

to be able to afford sth.	sich etw. leisten können
to blame sb.	jdm. die Schuld geben
button	Knopf
How dare you!	Was erlauben Sie sich!
tear	Träne
by mistake	aus Versehen

Johnson has taken her son in her arms now and is hurrying down the stairs.
"And you **blame** Richard Battlebolt. He's rich and successful, and he left you with nothing in life. It's normal that you hate him."
"Hate him? I've never..." Johnson hesitates for a second. "I've never met the man."
"Never? No email contact, no phone calls?"

They are in the street now, walking towards the underground station. The wind is blowing Johnson's short brown hair in her face. Her young son is playing with a button on her coat.
"No!" she pulls Alfie closer. "Who are you, anyway?"
"As I said before, my name is Charles Steede. I'm a private detective. I know all about the blackmail letters. And I know you're not telling the whole truth."

Exercise 16: Match up the words. **Bilden Sie zusammengesetzte Begriffe!**

1. ☐	underground	a) crash
2. ☐	blackmail	b) detective
3. ☐	car	c) letter
4. ☐	private	d) station

"What? How dare you!"
"If you *are* telling the truth, then you have no need to worry when I examine your phone call history. To see if you've contacted Battlebolt. If you're telling the truth..."
Steede doesn't end his sentence. He doesn't need to. There is a look of horror in Maria Johnson's face. Tears are forming in her eyes. Her bottom lip begins to shake. She looks away.
"I'm a part-time teacher and a full-time mother, Mr Steede. I work hard for my money. I'm a good person. Battlebolt isn't."
Steede nods.
"At first, I wanted to give my father a second chance to know me. And a chance to know his grandson. I got his mobile number and I rang him. He answered the call, but by mistake. He thought he'd ended

the call. But really, he'd accepted it. He was in the middle of a meeting with someone. And that someone, I realized, was the council planning officer. I heard everything. The size of the bribe. Every little detail. I was so angry. I didn't want this horrible, horrible man in my life."
"But you wanted to make him pay," Steede says. "You wanted to force him to support you and your son. And you wanted to protect the people of Islington from him. Battlebolt would be a terrible MP. Your friend Lindsay Farnham, on the other hand, would be an excellent MP. You convinced yourself that blackmailing your own father was a righteous act."
Maria Johnson stares at Steede.
Steede sighs. "And I'm not going to say you were wrong."

Some time later, Steede has told the whole story to Richard Battlebolt. Battlebolt takes a sip of whisky from his glass.
"I didn't know her mother was dead. I didn't know she had a son. I didn't know about any of this."

Exercise 17: Mistakes. Lesen Sie weiter und korrigieren Sie die sechs Fehler im Satz!

"Because you didn't want to no, Mr Battlebolt. You hat the chance too look for you're daughter and find out about her live. But you didnt."

Steede and Nug are standing in the living room of Richard Battlebolt's luxury villa. The millionaire looks even more pathetic than Nug expected.
"Excuse me, Mr Steede. I'm paying you for your detective skills, not for your morals and opinions." He takes another sip of whisky. "We

know who it was now, don't we? Maria can't threaten me any more."
"Do you think so?" Nug asks. "I'm not sure Maria agrees."
"What? I've said I won't report her to the police! Isn't that enough? Or does she want me to **suffer** even more?"
"I don't think you understand, Mr Battlebolt. Maria's methods may be **questionable**, even wrong. But she makes a good point."
"I don't believe what I'm hearing," Battlebolt **hisses**. "You think I should step down as a candidate in the election? What does she know about politics! She's a photography teacher. She doesn't have a clue if I'll make a good MP or not!"

horrible	schrecklich, grausam
righteous	gerecht
pathetic	erbärmlich, jämmerlich, armselig
to suffer	leiden
questionable	fragwürdig
to hiss	fauchen
otherwise	sonst

"Okay, she hasn't studied politics, but she knows a lot more about the day-to-day life of the people of Islington than you do!" says Nug.
"I don't think Maria will go to the newspapers and create a scandal," Steede adds. "But I do think the people of Islington have a right to know the truth about election candidates. It's essential for democracy."
"But you... what? What are you saying?!"
"In fact, I would say it is my responsibility to inform the people of Islington. How would I sleep at night, if I knew a corrupt, heartless millionaire was in power?"
"You... you..."
"Step down from the election campaign," Nug says. "And provide your daughter and grandson with the financial support they need. **Otherwise**..."
"Alright! Alright!" Battlebolt shouts angrily. "I hope you two are happy with your work," he adds, sarcastically.
Nug puts his hat on and turns to his partner and smiles.
"Just another day at the office."

Guided Murder

Gina Billy

1 The Boss Is Not Always Right

The phone on Sheila Stone's desk at Armstrong House begins ringing. She answers the call in her best professional voice.

"Good morning. My Lord and Lady Tours. Sheila Stone speaking, how may I help you?"

"Hello, darling. It's me, your fiancé."

"Oh, Gordon, it's lovely to hear your voice. But I can't talk now."

"Is the boss there?" Gordon asks.

"Yes. He's in his office."

"Listen, Sheila, I just want to check that everything is ready for the welcome tea at four o'clock. My group from Germany is really excited about it. Is Lord Lawrence going to be there?"

voice	Stimme
fiancé/fiancée	Verlobter/Verlobte
to whisper	flüstern
to offer	anbieten
guided tour	Führung
ϟ Bloody hell!	Verdammt!
to contrast with	*hier*: ergänzen

"Yes, I think so. But he's not happy about it."

Just then the door next to Sheila's little office opens.

"I think he wants something," she whispers. "I have to go."

"Sheila, come in here right now!"

The loud voice coming from her boss's office makes Sheila Stone close her eyes. When she opens them again, she sees all the work waiting on her desk. She has so many things to do this Monday morning. Business at My Lord and Lady Tours is going very, very well. The company offers special, guided tours to visitors to London. The tourists come from all over the world. Part of Sheila's job is to make sure that all of them have a great time. The other part is to try and keep her new boss, Lord Lawrence Armstrong, happy. This is the part of her job that Sheila hates.

"Sheila, where the **bloody hell** are you?"

"I'm coming, Lord Lawrence. I'm coming."

Sheila stands up and quickly checks her clothes. She's wearing a new outfit. The brown skirt and jacket look good on her. They **contrast** nicely **with** her golden-blonde hair and dark-blue eyes. But maybe the skirt is a little short for the office. Sheila pulls it down a bit. Now she's ready.

Exercise 1: Choose the right word. Lesen Sie weiter und unterstreichen Sie das richtige Wort!

Sheila walks into Lord Lawrence's **1.** bureau / office, which is much bigger than hers. It has a **2.** site / view to the nearby Kensington Gardens. Her **3.** boss / chef is sitting in a black, leather **4.** stool / chair in front of the large windows and is looking outside. Sheila cannot see his face but she doesn't **5.** think / mean that he is enjoying himself. She is pretty sure that Lord Lawrence is in a bad **6.** feeling / mood – again. Sheila takes a deep breath.

"What can I do for you, sir?" she asks friendly.
"First of all, when I call you, I expect you to come **at once** – not five minutes later! And secondly, I want to tell you that I am stopping this business of welcome teas for our tour guests. The teas are too expensive and **waste** my time."

> Als **high tea** bezeichnet man eine Mahlzeit zwischen 18 und 19 Uhr, die nur zu besonderen Anlässen eingenommen wird. Es handelt sich um einen Imbiss, zu dem Tee getrunken wird und der am **high table**, dem Esstisch, serviert wird.

"But, Lord Lawrence, the guests just love having high tea here and then seeing Armstrong House and the gardens. This is something our **competitors** don't have and it makes our company even more special. Your mother, Lady Melissa, always says..."
"My mother does not run the company any more," he shouts. "You work for me now, not for my mother. Do you understand?"
"Yes, sir. Of course, sir."
Sheila's voice stays calm. But inside, she's very angry.
It really is **too bad** that Lady Melissa **retired** and let her only son have the business. Lord Lawrence is not a good boss.
"Now, about this tea," he says. "I suppose I will have to come today. But this is the last one. **Unless**, of course, you find a way to make me **change my mind**."
Lord Lawrence's voice now sounds much quieter. The look in his brown eyes makes Sheila nervous.
"I don't understand, sir."

at once	sofort, gleich
to waste	verschwenden
competitor	Konkurrent
too bad	ein Jammer
to retire	in Ruhestand gehen
unless	es sei denn
to change one's mind	seine Meinung ändern
to fire sb.	feuern, jmd. entlassen
salary	Gehalt
nastily	fies, gemein

Even as Sheila says the words, she knows they aren't true. She has a very good idea of where this conversation is going. It's not the first time.
"Let me put it like this. If you are nice to me, I will be nice to you – and to your over-qualified fiancé Gordon Richards."
Lord Lawrence stands up and comes towards Sheila. He's standing very close to her when he says his next words.
"I'm thinking about firing Gordon. These days, it's easy to find tour guides who will work cheaply. Gordon's high salary costs the company a lot of money. He earns too much."
"But, Lord Lawrence, Gordon is wonderful at his job and..."
"I'm the boss, Sheila, and the boss is always right."
"Well, well, well. What's going on here? A little private meeting between boss and secretary?"
The woman now standing in the office door smiles nastily at her husband and Sheila.
"I mean personal assistant," the woman adds sarcastically.

Exercise 2: Contracted forms. **Schreiben Sie die Kurzformen der hervorgehobenen Wörter auf!**

1. Lord Lawrence **does not** like the teas. ____________
2. He thinks **they are** too expensive. ____________
3. "One minute, **I am** coming!" she says. ____________
4. **She will** go back to her desk. ____________

"No, Glenda, my dear." Lord Lawrence smiles back nastily at his wife. "Sheila and I are just talking about the tea this afternoon. Are you planning to be there, too?"

Glenda Smyth-Armstrong pushes her long, perfectly styled red hair back from her face with a well-manicured finger.
"Oh, darling, I wouldn't miss teatime with you and the tourists for all the money in the world."
"Well, Lord Armstrong, if that's all, I'll get back to my desk now. Please excuse me," Sheila says and uses her chance to **escape**.
Lady Glenda waits until Sheila closes the door. Then she starts shouting at her husband.
"Lawrence, you have more important things to do than flirt with an **employee**. You need to focus on what you are going to do about Kyle Simmons before you meet him this afternoon."
"What do you know about my business with Kyle?"
Now Lord Lawrence sounds a bit nervous.
"I know that you are in big trouble with him and that he is a dangerous man."
Lady Glenda starts whispering and Sheila can't hear her next words. Sheila **wonders** what's going on. Normally she makes all Lord Lawrence's **appointments** for him, but she doesn't know about any meeting with Kyle Simmons. Then she looks at her watch and decides to make a quick phone call to Gordon. She doesn't see that another woman is coming up to the front door of the office. It's Barbara Reynolds. She is Lady Melissa's much younger cousin, who also works at the tour company. Barbara starts to open the door, but stops when she hears Sheila talking.
"Gordon, where are you now?"
"I'm at the British Museum with the German group."
"Oh, well, I don't want to **disturb** you, it's just..."
"Sheila, you don't sound good. Is everything okay?"
"No, not really. Things are just **awful** here today."
"What's wrong, darling?"
"Lord Lawrence and Lady Glenda are having a terrible **row** – again... and before that, he, he..."

"He what?" Gordon asks.
"Oh **never mind**, it's just... sometimes I wish, I wish..."
"What do you wish, Sheila?"
"I just wish Lord Lawrence would go away... permanently."
"Do you mean what I think you do? Because if it's the plan we sometimes talk about, there could be a way to make it happen."
"Really, Gordon? Oh that sounds **too good to be true**. But let's not talk about it on the phone. Let's discuss it later, okay?"
"Okay."
Sheila tells Gordon that she loves him and puts down the phone.
Barbara Reynolds smiles to herself. Then she pushes the door all the way open and walks inside.
"Good morning, Sheila," she says. "How are you today?"
"Oh, hello Barbara. I'm okay, and you?"

to escape	entkommen
employee	Angestellte
to wonder	sich fragen
appointment	Termin
to disturb sb.	jmd. stören
awful	schrecklich
row	Streit
never mind	Schon gut!, Vergiss es!
too good to be true	zu schön um wahr zu sein
to keep sb.	jmd. aufhalten

Just then, Lady Glenda comes out of the other door and closes it loudly. She looks very unhappy. But her face changes when she sees Barbara standing by the door.
"Oh Barbara, are you still working here? It must be so hard for you now that Lawrence is the boss."
Barbara just smiles sweetly at Lady Glenda and says, "Glenda, dear, how very nice of you to think about my feelings. But please, don't let us **keep** you. I'm sure you have much more important business to do. Things like buying new shoes or having lunch."
Glenda smiles back at Barbara. "Yes, you're right. Talking with you is a waste of time. But Sheila..."
"Yes, Lady Glenda?"

"I have a message for you from my husband. He's expecting Mr Simmons at three o'clock this afternoon. Until then, he doesn't want anyone to disturb him. Is that clear?"
"Of course, Lady Glenda."

Exercise 3: Relationship matching. Ordnen Sie den Charakteren die richtige Beziehung zu!

1. ☐ Sheila Stone
2. ☐ Lawrence Armstrong
3. ☐ Lady Melissa
4. ☐ Barbara Reynolds

a) Lawrence's mother

b) Melissa's cousin

c) Gordon's fiancé

d) Glenda's husband

Lady Glenda **leans across** Sheila's desk and speaks very softly. "And Sheila, I have a little message for you, too. I'm not blind. I can see how he looks at you. But men will be men. It's your job to make sure that you two only have a professional relationship."
Now Sheila isn't just angry – she's **furious**. She opens her lips to say something nasty, but Lady Glenda stops her.
"Now, now Sheila, don't **lose your temper**."
Lady Glenda walks towards the door and Barbara moves away from it. But Lady Glenda isn't finished.

"Oh, and Sheila, you really should wear longer skirts to work. It just doesn't look … professional."

to lean across	sich herüber beugen
furious	wütend, bitterböse
to lose one's temper	die Beherrschung verlieren

Now Sheila feels like she is going to explode. "You can't speak to me like that! You're not my employer!" But Lady Glenda is finally gone. "Well, Sheila," Barbara says, "I hate to tell you this, but Lady Glenda can say and do anything she wants. At My Lord and Lady Tours, the boss's wife is always right."

2 The Late Boss

"On the right, Ladies and Gentleman, you can see the famous Hyde Park. It's the largest park in London's centre."

The tourists riding in the bus are listening carefully to Gordon.

"Are we stopping here?" asks Petra Berkl. "I really want to see Speaker's Corner – and the Princess Diana **Memorial Fountain**."

"No, Petra, we don't have time now. We're almost at Armstrong House. But we'll come back later."

Gordon then tells them they are now passing Kensington Gardens. A few minutes later, the coach stops in front of a very big, beautiful building across from the Gardens.

late	*hier*: verstorben
Memorial Fountain	Gedenkbrunnen
staff	Mitarbeiter, Personal
Mind the step!	Vorsicht Stufe!
to race	rasen
drive	Auffahrt
Assistant Manager	Direktionsassistent
library	Bibliothek
pleasure	Freude
to introduce sb.	jmd. vorstellen, bekanntmachen

"All right, everyone. Here we are. I hope you are all hungry – and thirsty! Lord Armstrong and his **staff** have a lovely tea waiting for you. Now **mind the step!**"

Gordon steps outside and turns to help one of the older tourists exit the coach. It's Petra. But suddenly, a black limousine **races** around the corner. It almost hits Gordon and Petra.

"Petra, are you all right?" Gordon asks.

"Fine, Gordon, just fine," she answers. "But London drivers are very fast! My nerves could really use a cup of tea now!"

The rest of the tourists get off the coach and all of them walk up the short drive leading to the house. Barbara Reynolds opens the door. "Good afternoon, everyone! Welcome to London and Armstrong House. I'm Barbara Reynolds, the Assistant Manager of My Lord and Lady Tours. Please come in."
Barbara leads the group through the entrance hall. Gordon whispers something to her. Then he leaves and goes in another direction. Barbara starts talking about Armstrong House and its history.
"And this is the library. The glass doors at the other end open to a large terrace. Because the weather is so fine today, that's where we'll have our tea."
The terrace has many small tables and lots of comfortable-looking chairs. Each table has a tea service and silver plates filled with biscuits, cake and little sandwiches. Barbara tells everyone to please have a seat.
Just then, Sheila and a woman with short, grey hair come through the doors. Barbara is surprised to see her cousin.

Exercise 4: Pronouns. **Lesen Sie weiter und setzen Sie die richtigen Pronomen ein!**

us | me | you | my | our | myself

"Oh Lady Melissa, it's lovely that 1. ______ are joining 2. ______ today. This is an unexpected pleasure for 3. ______ guests. Let 4. ______ introduce you."
"Yes, well, I can do that 5. ______, Barbara. I always enjoy meeting our visitors. But where is 6. ______ son?"

"Isn't Lawrence here, yet?" Now Lady Glenda is standing at the doors and Gordon is right behind her.
"I'll go back across to the office and get him," Sheila offers. "His meeting with Mr Simmons should be finished by now."
Lady Glenda gives Sheila a hard look. "No. I'm his wife, so I'll go and find him. Sheila, why don't you and Barbara serve the tea?"
Lady Glenda goes back through the library. Then Sheila and Barbara begin **pouring** tea for the tourists. It is very pleasant sitting in the afternoon sunshine, drinking tea and making small talk. Everyone looks as if they are having a very nice time. Petra Berkl asks Lady Melissa about the beautiful woman who is looking for Lord Lawrence.
"That's Lady Glenda Smyth-Armstrong, my son's wife."
Petra looks a little surprised to hear this, but she doesn't have time to ask any more questions.
Suddenly, the lovely high tea is **interrupted** by a woman's screams. It's Glenda, and she's running back onto the terrace.
"Help, please help me," she shouts. "It's Lawrence and..."
Tears are running down Glenda's face and she can't speak.
Gordon jumps up from his chair. "Glen ... Lady Glenda, what is it? Calm down and try to tell us what's wrong."
Lady Glenda takes a deep breath.
"Lawrence is at his desk and... and he's covered in blood!"
Her words are shocking, **especially** for Lady Melissa. Her tea cup smashes on the ground. This makes everyone even more nervous.

to pour	*hier*: einschenken
to interrupt	unterbrechen
tear	Träne
especially	besonders
ambulance	Krankenwagen
to rush off	forteilen
There, there!	*tröstende Worte*
perhaps	vielleicht
injured	verletzt
horrible	schrecklich, grausam
to bear to do sth.	es ertragen, etw. zu tun

"Glenda, is he still alive? Or is he, is he..." Lady Melissa can't make herself say the word everyone is thinking.
"Dead. I think he's dead. Please, somebody do something." Lady Glenda is almost hysterical now.
Barbara is the only person who stays calm. "Gordon, come with me. And Sheila, call for an **ambulance**."
Sheila runs at once to the phone in the library, and Barbara and Gordon head quickly towards Lord Lawrence's office.
"Wait," says Melissa, "I want to come with you."
But Barbara doesn't think that is a good idea.
"I know you're worried, Melissa, but please wait here. If Lady Glenda is right, you can't help Lawrence now. I'll come back as soon as I know more."
As they **rush off**, Petra puts an arm around Lady Melissa.
"**There, there**, dear. Try and hope for the best. **Perhaps** Lady Glenda is wrong and your son is only **injured**."
Lady Glenda starts crying again.

Exercise 5: Opposites. Lesen Sie weiter und unterstreichen Sie die Gegenteile der angegebenen Wörter!

hot | happily | wonderful | light | full | closed

"No, I'm so sorry Melissa," she says sadly. "His eyes are open, but they look so cold and empty. And there's all that dark blood.
It's just too **horrible**. I couldn't **bear to** touch him. But I don't think he's breathing any more."

Now Lady Melissa is crying, too. But her tears are silent and she can hear Sheila talking on the phone in the library.

"Yes. That's right. A medical **emergency** at Armstrong House in Kensington. Please, **hurry**."

Just as Sheila is ending the call, Gordon comes back. Sheila can tell by the look on his face that the news isn't good.

"Sheila, it's too late for a doctor," he whispers. "You have got what you want. Lord Lawrence is gone **for good**."

"What do you mean?" Sheila is whispering too.

"He really is dead. Call the police."

"The police! Gordon, are you sure?"

"Yes, something is sticking out of Lord Lawrence's **chest**. It looks like his **paper knife**, and I don't think he put it there himself. I'm afraid[i] that means murder."

"Murder! Gordon, how do you know that? Don't tell me you...?"

"Sheila, be quiet! How can you think such a thing? Just call the police – now! I have to tell his family and **take care of** the group."

"All right, I'll do it. But where's Barbara?"

"She's making sure no one comes into the office and disturbs anything. It's a crime scene now."

Out on the terrace, Lady Melissa is still at the table with Petra. Lady Glenda is sitting with them now, but she's just staring **blankly** at her

emergency	Notfall
to hurry	sich beeilen
for good	endgültig
chest	Brust(korb)
paper knife	Brieföffner
to take care of sb.	sich um jmd. kümmern
blankly	ausdruckslos

> **Afraid** wird hier nicht in der Bedeutung „Angst haben" verwendet, sondern bedeutet „befürchten".

hands. The tourists are speaking quietly together, but they all stop talking when Gordon comes back outside.

"Lady Melissa, I'm so terribly sorry. Perhaps you and Lady Glenda should come with me to a more private room."

Lady Melissa shakes her head. "No, Gordon. Tell me now. It's the not knowing that is killing me."

So Gordon does as she asks. The news that Lord Lawrence is dead isn't really a surprise any more. The shock comes when Gordon says that the death looks like **foul play**.

foul play	Verbrechen
to turn pale	blass werden
upset	durcheinander, aufgebracht

"But I don't understand," Lady Melissa says. "Who could do such a thing? Lawrence is such a wonderful man. Why would anyone want to kill him?"

Gordon can think of a million answers to that question, but he doesn't say them.

"I don't know, Lady Melissa. Those are questions for the police. Sheila's calling them now. They should arrive soon."

Lady Glenda's face **turns pale** when she hears the word 'police'. She turns to her mother-in-law and says, "Excuse me, Melissa, I um, I need a few minutes alone."

Glenda practically runs from the terrace to the library. She gets there just as Sheila is finishing the call to the police.

"Lady Glenda, I'm so very sorry about Lord Lawrence. Is there anything I can do for you?"

"Just get out of my way, you little bitch. I'm sure you are sorry, but not as sorry as you will be."

"Lady Glenda, I know you're **upset**, but really..."

The loud ringing of the front door bell interrupts Sheila's words. Glenda jumps at the sound.

"Is that the police?" she asks.

Exercise 6: Past tense verbs. Ergänzen Sie die Simple Past Form der folgenden Verben!

1. want ____________________
2. say ____________________
3. do ____________________
4. have ____________________
5. stand ____________________

"No, there's no way they could get here so soon. It must be the ambulance. I'll go and let them in."

As soon as Sheila leaves the library, Lady Glenda picks up the phone. She doesn't have much time. She quickly punches in a number and waits impatiently for someone to answer.

impatiently — ungeduldig

When he does, Glenda whispers a few words. She finishes with, "Goodbye, Kyle."

She doesn't see that Petra is now standing at the terrace doors.

Hm, Petra thinks. This trip to London is turning out to be a very, very interesting one.

3 Nobody Liked the Boss

An hour later, Armstrong House is filled with police officers and members of the forensic team. Two Detective Inspectors, or DIs, from the Metropolitan Police are questioning Lord Lawrence's family and employees in the library. Another officer is sitting with the German tourists outside on the terrace.

forensic	gerichtsmedizinisch
to examine	untersuchen
dagger	Dolch
case	(Kriminal-)Fall
weapon	Waffe

Over in Lord Lawrence's office, the forensic team leader is just finishing her first examination of the body. Dr April Rivers takes another photograph of the paper knife sticking out of the body. Then she slowly pulls it out so she can examine it more closely. It's shaped like a dagger.

Now that's interesting, Dr Rivers says to herself.

Just then, Detective Inspector Aldo Miller comes into the office. Because they have worked on so many murder cases together, DI Miller and Dr Rivers know each other very well.

"What can you tell me so far, April?" DI Miller asks her.

"Well, Aldo, I have to do the standard tests first, but it looks like the time of death was only a couple of hours ago. One thing I know for sure is that he didn't kill himself."

"How do you know?"

"Because the murder weapon is missing!"

"But April, you're holding it in your hand!"
Dr Rivers shakes her head and points the dagger playfully at him.
"You mean this? Well, it was in the victim's chest, but this isn't what killed him."
She puts the dagger into a plastic bag. Then she pulls open Lord Lawrence's blood-covered shirt.
"Look here, Aldo, the wound is a little bigger and deeper than this paper knife could make."
"And that means?"

victim	Opfer
to stab	erstechen
thank goodness	Gott sei Dank!
to be on first name terms	per du sein
none of your business	das geht dich nichts an
to take statements	Aussagen aufnehmen

"It means somebody stabbed him with something else – a knife or maybe a scalpel. Then Lord Lawrence's killer put the paper knife in the wound."
"I wonder why?"
"Well, Aldo, that's your job, thank goodness, and not mine."
"Thanks, April. That's very helpful information. How long will you need for the autopsy?"
"Oh Aldo, you're always in such a hurry! I'll try my best to have it done by tomorrow afternoon."
"Perfect, April. Right. I'll just go back and see how Heather is managing with the interviews."
"How interesting! So the two of you are on first name terms now?" Dr Rivers says with a little laugh.
"That, April, is none of your business. Now, let's get back to work."
DI Miller leaves April with the body. His colleague, DI Heather Jones, is new to the Murder Investigation Team, or MIT. DI Miller thinks she's doing a good job so far.
When he gets back to the library, she's taking statements from Lord Lawrence's family and employees. Miller joins them and signals DI Jones to continue with the questioning.

Exercise 7: Question words. **Lesen Sie weiter und ergänzen Sie mit dem fehlenden Fragewort!**

"Lady Glenda," she asks, " 1. ________ was the last time you saw your husband alive?"

"I think it was around 10:30 this morning."

" 2. ________ did you see him?"

"In his office. We only talked for a few minutes and then I left."

" 3. ________ did you do after that?"

"I was shopping and then I had lunch with a friend," she replies. " 4. ________ is this important?"

Lady Glenda suddenly looks a little scared. DI Jones smiles at her and tells her these are just standard questions.

"And Lady Glenda, did your husband have any **enemies**?"

"No, not that I know of. Everybody liked Lawrence. He is – was a wonderful man."

enemy	Feind
expression	Ausdruck

Sheila almost laughs out loud when she hears this. And Gordon and Barbara both have sceptical **expressions** on their faces. The two DIs notice that the atmosphere has changed. Before they can ask more questions, Lady Glenda starts crying again.

"I'm sorry, Lady Glenda," Jones says. "I know this must be hard for you. But we are trying to find your husband's killer."
"Oh, you don't have to be sorry for Lady Glenda," Sheila interrupts. "She hated her husband! I'm sure she's very glad he's dead. Maybe she even killed him herself!"
At Sheila's words, everyone starts talking at the same time.
"How dare you!" Lady Glenda screams.
"Sheila, how can you say such a thing?" Lady Melissa cries.
Gordon jumps up and says, "Sheila, that's crazy!"
"You hated him, too," Barbara shouts.
"So did you! You wanted his job! Everybody hated him," Sheila shouts back. "He was a horrible man!"
The situation is loud and chaotic. DI Miller slams his hand down hard on the table and everyone is suddenly quiet again.
"Now calm down, everyone. I'm stopping this group interview right now. We'll take a break for a few minutes. After that, DI Jones and I will talk to each of you again."

Exercise 8: Fill in the blanks. **Lesen Sie weiter und setzen Sie die angegebene Präpositionen richtig ein!**

towards | on | up | with | outside | at

DI Miller stands **1.** ________ and asks DI Jones to come **2.** ________ him. They walk **3.** ________ the terrace and leave the others **4.** ________ the table. Before they go **5.** ________, DI Jones puts her hand **6.** ________ Miller's arm.

"But Aldo, why did you do that?" Heather whispers to him. "Things were just starting to get really interesting."

"I know. But we will find out more if we talk to each of them separately. And I need to tell you something important."

DI Miller gives his partner the surprising news about the murder weapon. While they are talking, Constable Steven Thompson leaves the German tourists alone for a second.

"Excuse me, DI Miller, DI Jones. What are we going to do with this lot?" he asks politely. "They say that they are tired and they're starting to get impatient. They have also got tickets for a musical in the West End tonight."

DI Miller sighs when he hears that. I wish I had time to go to the theatre, he thinks. That would be a nice thing to do with a pretty woman, someone like... Miller puts this unprofessional thought out of his head. Work has to come first.

"Did you take the tourists' statements?"

"No one told me to do that, sir. My orders were just to sit with them. But one of them wants to talk with you or DI Jones. Her name is Petra Berkl. She seems quite sensible. And she speaks very good English," Stevens adds.

How dare you!	Was fällt dir ein!
to slam	knallen
to take a break	Pause machen
ϟ lot	*hier*: Haufen, Pack
to sigh	seufzen
sensible	vernünftig
to imagine sth.	sich etw. vorstellen
crucial	entscheidend

DI Miller can't imagine how an ordinary[i] tourist could possibly help the investigation. They have so many other things to do right now – and there is absolutely no time to waste. The first few hours after a murder are the most crucial.

Ordinary heißt nicht etwa „ordinär", sondern „gewöhnlich".

"All right, Stevens, ask this Ms Berkl to wait a little longer. The other tourists can all leave. But make sure you get their names and contact details. Heather and I will get started with the one-on-one interviews."
"What's our plan, Aldo?" Heather asks. "Should we do the 'good cop/bad cop' routine?"
"Good idea, Heather. Let's start with Ms Sheila Stone. She seems to have a lot to say."

Exercise 9: Mixed verb forms! Lesen Sie weiter und setzen Sie die angegebenen Verben richtig ein!

sit | finish | rest | be | go | do

Sheila **1.** __________ have a lot to tell the detectives and she **2.** __________ not the only one. By the time the interviews are **3.** __________, the sun has **4.** __________ down. Only Miller and Jones are still **5.** __________ in the library. Lady Glenda, Lady Melissa and Barbara are **6.** __________ upstairs. Sheila and Gordon are on their way home.

one-on-one	Einzel...
good cop/bad cop	guter Bulle/ böser Bulle
exhausted	erschöpft
valuable	wertvoll
suspect	Verdächtiger

They would all have to answer more questions tomorrow. Miller and Jones are both exhausted, but they are also happy. They now have lots of new and valuable information – and a suspect.

"So Heather, it looks like the only person who liked Lord Lawrence was his mother. What do you think? Who did it?"
"Well, any of them could have killed him. But **my money is on** Kyle Simmons. He has been in trouble with the police before. Just last week there was an article about him and his casino in the paper. It said that he has some dubious business connections. And we know from Sheila Stone and Lady Glenda that Simmons had a meeting with the victim this afternoon."
"Yes, but it's **strange** that Lady Glenda didn't tell us about it right away, isn't it?"
"Perhaps she was just in shock. Anyway, we will know more tomorrow. I think it's time we stopped for today."
"Um, **speaking of which**," said Miller a little nervously, "do you **fancy** an after-work beer at the next pub?"

↯ My money is on ...	*hier*: Ich tippe auf ...
strange	seltsam, merkwürdig
speaking of which	apropos
↯ to fancy	Lust haben auf
pint	*hier*: ein Bier (ca. 0,56 l)
homicide	Mord

"Well, I don't know about her, but I'm dying for a **pint**!"
The words coming from the terrace make the two DIs jump.
"Oh, you must be Ms Berkl," Heather says. "I'm so terribly sorry. Constable Stevens said you wanted to talk to us. I'm afraid we..."
"You forgot all about me. But don't worry. I know you are very busy – and murder investigations are very hard work."
"Yes, they are," Miller said. "But how do you know that?"
"Because when I'm not on holiday, I work as a **homicide** detective for the police in Berlin," she says with a smile.
At first, Miller and Jones just stare at her with their mouths open in surprise. Miller finds his voice first.
"Are you in London on business, or only for pleasure?"
"Well, I came here just for fun. But since murder is my business, I

guess it's both now. Invite me for a beer. There are a couple of things I saw and heard today you should know about."

Exercise 10: Translation. **Übersetzen Sie und enträtseln Sie das Lösungswort!**

1. Aussage ☐ _ _ _ _ _ _ _ _
2. Wunde _ _ ☐ _ _
3. Feinde _ _ _ _ _ _ ☐
4. Ausdruck _ _ ☐ _ _ _ _ _ _ _
5. vorstellen _ _ _ _ _ _ ☐
6. ängstlich _ ☐ _ _ _ _
7. erschöpft _ _ _ _ _ _ ☐ _ _

Lösung: _ _ _ _ _ _ _

4 The Casino Boss

"Cheers, Ms Berkl," Heather says and raises her glass of beer.
"Cheers! Oh, and please call me Petra."
"Thank you, Petra. I'm Heather and this is Aldo."
"Yes cheers, ladies! Now let's get down to business."
The three of them are sitting in a cosy pub near Hyde Park.

Let's get down to business.	Kommen wir zur Sache.
cosy	gemütlich
to run sb. over	jmd. überfahren
number plate	Autokennzeichen

"Petra, what can you tell us?" Aldo asks.
"Well, first of all, just as our group arrived at Armstrong House, a dark limousine raced away. It almost ran me over! I got the number on the number plates, though."

Exercise 11: Synonyms. **Ordnen Sie die Begriffe mit gleichen Bedeutungen einander zu!**

1. ☐ to contact — a) to lift
2. ☐ to raise — b) homicide
3. ☐ murder — c) to get in touch with
4. ☐ to follow up — d) to investigate

"That was clever, Petra. I'll have someone check the number right away. Excuse me for a second."

Heather takes out her mobile phone and calls the police station. While she's on the phone, Petra keeps talking to Aldo.

"The next thing is, I think Lady Glenda has some connection to your main suspect. She called someone only minutes after she found the body. I couldn't hear the conversation, but at the end she said 'Goodbye, Kyle'."

"Well, that does sound **suspicious**," Aldo tells her.

"And one more thing. I saw Lady Glenda around noon today at the British Museum. Our tour guide suddenly **disappeared** for a few minutes. However, I needed to use the ladies room, and when I went to find it, I saw Gordon and Lady Glenda. They were talking to each other."

suspicious	verdächtig
to disappear	verschwinden
clue	Hinweis, Anhaltspunkt
lead	(heiße) Spur
to follow sth. up	etw. nachverfolgen

"What? Lady Glenda and Gordon Richards? But he's..."

Just then Heather finishes her call. "Thanks very much."

Her grey eyes are bright with excitement. "Guess who owns the dark limousine?"

"Uh, I don't know. Could it be Mr Kyle Simmons maybe?" Aldo answers.

"Almost. It's a company car and belongs to his casino. Aldo, why don't we go there now? It's on Knightsbridge Road, not far from here. We can walk there in less than ten minutes."

Aldo thinks this is a good idea. The **clues** are pouring in now. He quickly tells Heather about the new **lead** on Gordon and Lady Glenda. They decide to **follow it up** first thing tomorrow.

"All right, Heather, let's go and pay Mr Simmons a visit. Petra, can we call you a taxi to take you somewhere?"

"Oh, can't I come with you?" Petra's eyes are excited.
"I'm sorry, Petra, but that's **against the rules**. Thank you so much for your help, though. Here's my business card. Contact us if you think of anything else."
"Yes, thanks, Petra. And enjoy the rest of your stay in London," Heather adds and the two women shake hands.

"Come on, Aldo. Let's go! Who knows, maybe we'll **get lucky** and can **solve** the case tonight!"
Sheila and Gordon are sitting at home eating dinner. It's very quiet in their small flat in Chelsea. They don't know what to say to each other. Sheila pours herself another glass of white wine. Then she sighs and asks Gordon if he wants one, too.
"Yes, darling. That would be lovely," he says, smiling at her tiredly. Now that the ice is broken, Sheila feels she can talk to him.
"Gordon, can I ask you something?"
"Of course, Sheila. You're the woman I am going to marry. You can ask me anything."

to be against the rules	gegen die Regeln verstoßen
to get lucky	Glück/Erfolg haben
to solve sth.	etw. lösen
serious	ernst

Sheila takes a deep breath. "Gordon, did you do it?"
"Do what, Sheila?"
"You know, what we talked about – I mean we were never **serious** about it, but..."
"Sheila, are you asking me if I stabbed Lord Lawrence?"
"Well, I know you didn't. It's just, well you could have done it – for me, or for us."
"Sheila, that's just crazy. I would never do something like that." Gordon isn't smiling any more. "And what about you, did you kill him?"
"Certainly not! He was still alive when I left the office to go and finish preparing things for the tea."

"Oh, it's silly for us to talk to each other like this," Gordon says. He gets up and takes Sheila in his arms. "Anyway, it really looks as if Kyle Simmons is the murderer. At least the police seem to think so." Gordon tries to kiss Sheila, but she pulls away.
"I'm sorry Gordon, I don't feel very well. It was an awful day. I think I'll have a shower and go to bed early. What about you?"
"I need to relax a little first. I'll clear the table and do the washing up. Then I think I'll watch the news. Sleep well, Sheila."
"You, too, Gordon. Good night."

Exercise 12: Adjective and adverbs. Lesen Sie weiter und bilden Sie sinnvolle Wörter aus dem Buchstabenchaos!

"Good evening, ladies, sir. How may I help you?" The **1.** ngeleta ___________ receptionist at the casino **2.** yelploit ___________ welcomes the new guests. But she's looking at them a little **3.** reglyasnt ___________. They aren't wearing evening dress like the other people at the **4.** uvelxices ___________ casino.
"We're here on **5.** tiamnprot ___________ police business," DI Miller says. Since he and DI Jones are wearing plainclothes, they both show her their badges.

The receptionist frowns and purses her bright red lips. "And may I ask what brings you here?"

She looks around to see if anyone else has noticed that the police are here.

"We would like to see your boss, Kyle Simmons. Is he here?"

"I'm not sure. Just a moment please. I'll see if he's available."

She turns her back on them to make a quick phone call. But in that moment, the detectives see not one, but two familiar faces. Kyle Simmons is coming into the casino. And Lady Glenda is holding his hand!

"This day is just full of surprises," Heather tells Aldo as they watch them enter the room.

evening dress	Abendkleidung
plainclothes *pl*	Zivilkleidung
badge	*hier*: Dienstmarke
to frown	die Stirn runzeln
to purse one's lips	den Mund spitzen
available	zur Verfügung stehen
handsome	gut aussehend
right	Recht
actually	in der Tat, eigentlich
to arrest sb.	jmd. verhaften
handcuffs *pl*	Handschellen

"Lady Glenda, I'm so glad to see you're feeling better," Aldo says sarcastically as he walks up to the couple.

"Won't you introduce me to your, um, friend?"

Lady Glenda and Kyle Simmons are shocked to see the police. They both turn around and try to leave. But the detectives are too quick for them. Heather and Aldo rush over and block the exit.

"Not so fast, you two," Aldo says. "Let's go somewhere where we can talk privately."

Kyle Simmons' handsome face now looks very angry. "I know my rights, officer. I don't have to talk to the police. Now please leave my casino."

"Actually, Mr Simmons, you do have to talk to us. You are a suspect in the murder case of Lord Lawrence Armstrong," Heather tells him calmly. "So, you can talk to us here, or we can arrest you now. Then all your guests can stare while we put handcuffs on you. After that, we will take you to the police station for questioning. It's your choice."

"Well, fine. There's no need to make a scene. Let's go up to my office. Glenda, I'll have my driver take you home."

At first, Lady Glenda can't decide what to do. But then a **determined** expression crosses her pretty face and she says, "No, Kyle. I want to stay with you."

"All right, Lady Glenda, you come with us, too," Heather says.

All four of them go upstairs to Kyle Simmons office. He goes directly to the bar behind his desk.

Exercise 13: Which word? Lesen Sie weiter und unterstreichen Sie die richtige Variante!

"I think I will just get **1.** myself / me a drink first," says Simmons.

"Does anyone else **2.** like / want one?"

"No, thanks. We're **on duty**," Aldo **3.** means / answers.

Lady Glenda **4.** says / tells that she wants one **5.** to / too, and Kyle pours out two glasses of whisky.

"So, Mr Simmons, please tell me," Heather begins, "what **6.** were / was your business with Lord Armstrong this afternoon?"

"Oh well, I don't want to **speak ill of the dead**, but Lawrence was not a good businessman. He owed me money. I wanted it back."

Aldo asks the next question. "But Lord Lawrence was a very **wealthy** man. I don't understand why he would borrow money from you. And even if he did, why wouldn't he pay you back?"

"Let me answer that, Kyle," Lady Glenda says softly. She drinks from her whisky before she continues. "Lawrence had big money problems. He lost a lot of his **inheritance** in the financial crisis. He also liked to **gamble**, but he wasn't good at it. He had huge **debts** here at the casino."

"Yes, well that just makes things look worse for your 'friend' Mr Simmons." Aldo now looks directly at the suspect. "Kyle Simmons, did you lose your temper and murder Lord Lawrence?"

determined	entschlossen
on duty	im Dienst
to speak ill of the dead	den Toten etw. Schlechtes nachsagen
wealthy	vermögend
inheritance	Erbe
to gamble	um Geld spielen
debts *pl*	Schulden
widow	Witwe

Kyle slams his glass down on his desk. "Certainly not! I'm not stupid. A dead man can't pay his debts!"

"But perhaps his **widow** can," Aldo suggests.

"Kyle didn't kill my husband!" Lady Glenda is practically shouting now. "I talked to Lawrence again after Kyle left this afternoon."

Aldo's voice get's louder, too. "That means you didn't tell us the truth earlier. Why did you lie to us? Did you do it, Lady Glenda?"

"No! And I didn't lie to you. You asked me when I *saw* my husband the last time. It was this morning. This afternoon, we spoke on the phone right after Kyle left. Lawrence was very upset – but he was alive and well."

Heather starts to ask Lady Glenda about her relationship with Gordon Richards. But Aldo signals her to stop.

"All right, Lady Glenda," he says. "You are giving Kyle Simmons an alibi. But you can be sure we will check your story carefully."

Aldo and Heather stand up to go. Just before they leave the room, Aldo turns again at the door.
"Mr Simmons, one more thing. I think you should ask Lady Glenda about her other boyfriend."
"What?" Kyle says and stares at Glenda.
"Oh, it's just that I hear Gordon Richards is a very good guide. Have a pleasant evening."

Exercise 14: True or false? **Kreuzen Sie die korrekten Aussagen an!**

1. Sheila and Gordon suspect each other. ❐
2. Heather, Aldo and Petra go to an uncomfortable pub. ❐
3. Heather and Aldo are wearing uniforms. ❐
4. Lord Lawrence was very wealthy. ❐

5 The Boss's Murder Guide

When Big Ben strikes 9:00 the next morning, Aldo and Heather are sitting in a conference room at the Kensington police station. They have so many things they need to follow up on. First, though, they finish updating the other members of their Murder Investigation Team.

to sum up	zusammenfassen
opportunity	Gelegenheit
witness	Zeuge/Zeugin
search warrant	Durchsuchungsbefehl
flat	Wohnung

"So, to sum up," Aldo tells them, "at the moment, we have three main suspects. Lady Glenda Armstrong and her two lovers, Kyle Simmons and Gordon Richards. All three of them have motives for killing Lord Lawrence."

"What about opportunity?" asks Constable Thompson.

Heather explains that, theoretically, any of the suspects could have done it. "We need to carefully question all the witnesses again. But our first priority today is to continue our search for the murder weapon. We got search warrants this morning for Richards' and Simmons' flats. Forensic teams are at both places now."

Just then, the phone in the conference room starts ringing. Aldo answers it immediately.

"DI Miller, speaking."

Aldo listens for a second to the voice at the other end. His eyes widen at the news he hears.

"What? You did? Where?" he asks excitedly.
A few seconds later, Aldo hangs up the phone and reports to the team. "That was Constable Poole. He and his search team have just found a knife in a cupboard at Gordon Richards' and Sheila Stone's flat. There's dried blood on it!"
"Is Richards there?" Heather asks.
"No, Sheila Stone let the search team inside. Then she left for work. She says that Richards is with the tour group at Westminster Abbey."
"So, sir, do we arrest him there?" asks Constable Thompson.
"No. It's too soon for an arrest. The knife does look suspicious," Aldo adds, "but first Dr Rivers needs to see it and tell us if it is the murder weapon. Forensics also has to do tests on the blood and check the knife for fingerprints."
"So what do we do?" Heather asks.

Exercise 15: Definitions. Ordnen Sie die Wörter der passenden Definition zu!

1. ☐	opportunity	a) new information
2. ☐	update	b) a person who sees something happen
3. ☐	immediately	c) a chance to do something
4. ☐	witness	d) at once

"I think it's time for the two of us to have a little talk with Gordon Richards. Besides, my last trip to Westminster Abbey was about five years ago. Come on, let's go sightseeing!"
Gordon is waiting outside Westminster Abbey with the German tourists. Their tour of the 700-year-old building will start in just a few

minutes. Gordon looks tired and pale. His voice shakes a little as he tells the group about the Abbey's rich history. But no one notices because the tourists are too busy whispering to each other about the murder. Only Petra Berkl is watching Gordon very carefully.

Suddenly his mobile phone rings. Gordon looks at the display and answers the call.

"Sheila. What is it?" he says **impatiently**.

impatiently	ungeduldig
Royal Wedding	königliche Hochzeit

Gordon's face turns even paler when he hears what Sheila has to say. "What? You let the police into our flat – and you left them alone there? No, of course I don't have anything to hide!"

Gordon tells Sheila that he can't talk any more now and shuts his phone angrily. He takes a deep breath. The tourists stop whispering. Everyone is staring at him. Gordon says he is sorry for the interruption and continues telling the group about the last **Royal Wedding** at Westminster.

Petra suddenly remembers the phone call she heard him make yesterday at the British Museum. I need to tell Heather and Aldo about that call, she thinks. It could be important.

Petra moves away from the group and takes out her own mobile phone and Aldo's business card. She quickly types in a text message:

Exercise 16: Past or present? Lesen Sie weiter und setzen Sie die Verben richtig ein!

"I completely **1.** forget ____________ to tell you. **2.** Hear ____________ G.R. **3.** speak ____________ on phone yesterday with S. S. about 'a plan' they sometimes

4. talk ___________ about and 'making it happen'. S.S. just 5. call ___________ G. again. I think they're 6. have ___________ problems. Good luck! P.B."

Petra 7. punch ___________ the send button and hopes that she's not too late.

At her desk in the tourist agency, Sheila Stone slowly puts down the phone. There is a strange little smile on her face.

Gordon sounds so upset, she thinks. I wonder...

Before she can finish the thought, the door to her office opens. It's Barbara Reynolds.

"Good morning, Sheila. How interesting to see you at your desk."

"What do you mean? I always start work at 9:00."

"Oh, I just thought you would call in sick, today. After all, yesterday was, well, a very hard one for you."

Sheila frowns. She's not sure what Barbara is trying to tell her.

"Oh, don't worry. Your little secret is safe with me – for now, at least."

Now Barbara is the one smiling strangely. "But," she continues, "the two of us need to have a little heart-to-heart about your future at My Lord and Lady Tours."

to call in sick	sich krank melden
to have a heart-to-heart	ein ernstes Gespräch haben
traffic	Verkehr
development	Entwicklung

The heavy morning traffic in London means Heather and Aldo can't drive very fast. They have time to talk about the latest developments during the trip to Westminster.

"Aldo, a couple of things are troubling me. First, do you think that Gordon Richards killed Lord Lawrence because of Lady Glenda?"
"I don't know. Love and money are often motives for murders."
"Yes, that's true. But if he did it, do you really think that Richards is stupid enough to hide the murder weapon in his own flat? He seems like an intelligent man."
"Killers often make stupid mistakes, Heather. That's why we catch most of them. But I know what you mean."
Just then Aldo's mobile phone makes the sound that tells him he has a new text message. He reads the text quickly then tells Heather what it says.

to whistle	pfeifen
to keep an eye on sb./sth.	jmd./etw. im Auge behalten
blame	Schuld

Heather **whistles** lightly when she hears Petra's message.
"Aldo, are you thinking what I'm thinking?"
"Yes, I am. Turn the car around, Heather. I'll text Petra to **keep an eye on** Richards. I think we need to see his loving fiancée first!"

"What do you mean about my future here, Barbara?" Sheila's voice is calm, but her heart is beating fast.
"Oh, Sheila, there's no need to play games with me. You left the terrace yesterday afternoon about 15 minutes before the tourists came for tea. I saw you go back to the office and I followed you."
"Yes, well, I just wanted to, um, check on something." Sheila's voice is starting to sound a little nervous now.
"You didn't tell the police, though, did you? They think you left the office when Kyle Simmons arrived and never saw Lawrence again. But that's not true, is it?"
"Of course it's true! Why would I lie to the police?"
"Well, Sheila, we both know the answer to that, don't we? You killed Lawrence – and you are doing your best to make sure Gordon gets the **blame** for it."

Barbara starts laughing nastily. "Did you kill Lawrence because you hated him? Or did you want to punish Gordon for his affair with Lady Glenda?"
"Barbara, I think you really need to see a doctor or something."

Exercise 17: Translation. **Lesen Sie weiter und fügen Sie die richtige Übersetzung ein!**

Sheila looks Barbara in the eye when she says this. But her 1. rechte Hand ____________ is moving slowly towards the top 2. Schublade ____________ of her desk. Barbara 3. sieht es nicht ____________. "To be honest, Sheila, I'm not sorry at all that Lawrence is 4. tot ____________. Now I can 5. endlich ____________ be the boss here. Lady Melissa gave me the job this morning."

"Congratulations, Barbara. You're the best choice for the job," Sheila replies.
"Yes, but unfortunately, I really am going to have to let you go. I need a personal assistant that I can, um, trust. I'm not sure it's good for business to have a cold-blooded killer in the office. Our tourists certainly don't need a murder guide!"
Sheila suddenly jumps up from behind her desk. She now has a small gun in her hand.
"Well, Barbara," Sheila says and points the gun directly at her new boss. "Perhaps you'd like to reconsider your decision to sack me. I must say, the bosses at My Lord and Lady Tours do seem to be

rather, um, unlucky this week, don't they? Now walk over to Lord Lawrence's, I mean your office. I think it's time for you to, um, have a little accident."

Barbara knows that if she does what Sheila says, she will almost certainly end up dead. But she doesn't have much choice. So she starts to do as Sheila asks. But just then, the two women hear loud knocking on the front office door.

Sheila puts a finger on her lips and signals Barbara to be quiet.

But Barbara panics and starts screaming. "Help, help! She has a gun! She's going to..."

The sound of the gun going off makes Barbara scream even louder. Blood is pouring from a wound in her right arm. The door crashes open and Aldo and Heather rush through it. They are both **unarmed**, but Aldo **tackles** Sheila from behind and pushes her to the floor. The gun goes off again, and this time Sheila has shot herself.

"Heather, call an ambulance. Quickly!" Aldo shouts.

He turns Sheila over and tries to stop the blood from flowing out of her chest. She opens her eyes and tries to smile.

"Tell Gordon I'm sorry," she whispers. "I really did love him but..."

Sheila can't finish. Her eyes close again and she's gone.

to punish	bestrafen
to let sb. go	*hier*: jmd. entlassen, feuern
to trust	vertrauen
to reconsider	überdenken
ϟ to sack sb.	jmd. rausschmeißen, entlassen
unarmed	unbewaffnet
to tackle	angreifen, sich stürzen auf

Breathlessly Beautiful

Joseph Sykes

1 Romeo and Juliet

"So, who's your favourite pop star?" the man asks the girl.
"*Pop* star?" She looks at him, annoyed.
"What?" he asks. "Don't you like pop music? I do."
"Yes, I do, too. I just thought... Well, I *am* eighteen. You can talk to me about other things. Adult stuff, you know?"
"Adult stuff?" the man says, and smiles.
He offers the girl his hand and she takes it. The pair continue to walk up the Great Orme. From the hill, they can see the town of Llandudno[i] below and the island of Anglesey in the distance.

> Die Aussprache walisischer Namen ist oft schwierig. **Llandudno** wird „Chlan-did-no" ausgesprochen, **Rhys** spricht man „Ries", **Rhiannon** „Rie-ann-on" und **Cerys** „Keriss".

"So what kind of 'adult stuff' do you like to talk about?"
"You know..." she says, and then stops to think. What do adults talk about? "The weather?"
The man really starts to laugh now. It wasn't a joke, she thinks, but he must think it was. And that's okay. He looks even fitter with a big smile on his face. This thought makes her smile, too.
Out at sea, there are several big ships. She can see Llandudno beach and a few little dots of colour: people walking in the sand. It is still spring, so it's too cold for sunbathing and swimming. However, in a month or two the masses of tourists will arrive and fill the beach. Or, the girl thinks, it'll rain every day of the summer holidays and the seafront will stay empty.

"So, were you born around here?" the man asks.

He **scratches** his **designer stubble** and pulls his **beanie** over his thick brown hair.

annoyed	genervt
ϟ **adult stuff**	*hier*: erwachsene Themen
to offer	anbieten
ϟ **fit**	sexy, attraktiv
dot	Punkt
to scratch sth.	etw. kratzen
designer stubble	Dreitagebart
beanie	(Beanie-) Mütze

"No," the girl replies. "We moved to Llandudno six years ago. I was born in Criccieth. It's a seaside town in North Wales, like Llandudno, but much smaller. Have you heard of it?"

"Yes," the man says, and **nods** his head. "I think so. What was it like being a kid in a little place like Criccieth?"

"All right," she says.

What a boring thing to say, she thinks to herself. Can't you think of something more interesting? Something **mature**? He mustn't find out you're a young, naive girl. Today you're 18. Don't act like a schoolgirl.

to nod	nicken
mature	reif
awkward	verlegen, peinlich
cable car	Seilbahn
summit	Gipfel
emphasis	Betonung

For ten seconds they don't say anything. Now it's been fifteen seconds. Twenty. An **awkward** silence.

Oh no, she thinks to herself. Keep him interested!

Clank, clank, clank! A **cable car** passes above their heads. It is taking a group from Happy Valley in Llandudno to the **summit** of the Great Orme, the highest point in the town.

"Did you know the Llandudno cable car system is the longest in the UK?" she says. "I learnt that back when I was at school."

Too much **emphasis** on 'when I was at school', she tells herself. Don't tell even more lies. Just act like an 18-year-old.

"Really?" the man replies.
He raises his eyebrows. She notices his eyebrow piercing, again, and thinks 'That's really cool', again.
"We could climb to the top of the Great Orme and take the cable car back down to Happy Valley... if you want?" she suggests.
"All right," the man replies and smiles. "But let's lie in the sunshine for a while first. You know, there's no one else around. Only you and me." He smiles again and she sits down with him.
"Oh, but... Actually, it's, erm, 4:30," she says nervously. "I think the cable car closes soon. So maybe we should..."
"Ssshhh," he puts his finger to her lips. "We both know why we came up here. Me, you, the open sky?"
She looks into his eyes and doesn't know what to say.
"And we're both adults," he whispers. "Aren't we?"
She opens her mouth to speak, but he is already kissing her.

Exercise 1: Match up the words. Bilden Sie zusammengesetzte Begriffe!

1.	☐ eyebrow	a)	stubble
2.	☐ designer	b)	town
3.	☐ highest	c)	piercing
4.	☐ seaside	d)	point

Clank, clank, clank! The thousandth empty cable car of the day arrives at the lower cable car station in Happy Valley.
Or maybe the millionth, Simon Holland thinks. It certainly feels like it on a long, boring day at work, like today.
"Where are all the tourists?" his brother, Peter, asks. "I don't under-

stand. It's a beautiful day. It's the weekend. There should be a long queue of people for the cable car. I hope it doesn't continue like this in the summer. They won't need two cable car station attendants with so few tourists. You'll lose your job."

eyebrow	Augenbraue
actually	in der Tat, eigentlich
to whisper	flüstern
queue	Warteschlange
attendant	Aufseher
to lose	verlieren
ϟ Whatever!	Egal!
closing time	Feierabend
witty	schlagfertig
confused	verwirrt
shortly	gleich, in Kürze

"How many cars pass through this station every day?" Simon asks. "One arrives every ten or fifteen seconds, so... Wait a minute – *I'll* lose my job? I don't think so! *You'll* lose your job."

"Whatever," Peter replies. "Anyway, it's 4:55. Almost closing time. You can stay here doing your cable car maths, but I'm going to the pub with Rhys."

Simon considers a reply, but he isn't as witty as his older brother. Peter and their colleague, Rhys, often laugh at 'slow Simon'. And poor Simon just accepts it. Peter and Rhys are his only real friends.

Peter's phone starts to ring.

"This is Rhys now," he tells Simon, and then answers his phone. "Hello, Mr Matthews! How is life as an upper cable car station attendant?" he asks in a sarcastic tone.

"Oh, fantastic! I'm just calling to tell you that Romeo and Juliet will be with you in ten minutes."

"What?" Peter asks, confused by Rhys's comment.

"Yes, Romeo and Juliet are about to leave the upper station but will be with you shortly, and then you can close. See you later!"

Peter hangs up and turns to his brother. "Rhys said 'Romeo and Juliet' are about to come down. What do you think he means?"

"It'll be a Spanish couple on holiday here!" laughs Simon.

"Spanish?! Romeo and Juliet were Italian, you idiot! Anyway, I **reckon** it's just a fit girl and her boyfriend. Rhys probably couldn't take his eyes off her. You know what he's like with women!"
Simon doesn't want to laugh at his brother's comment, but he can't help it. It's true, he thinks. Rhys talks about women as much as he talks about himself – which is a lot.
Peter goes into the office and puts the money in the safe. He then goes outside and closes the gate to the station. A group of Japanese tourists are just arriving. He holds up his hands. "Sorry, we're closed."

Exercise 2: Verbs. Lesen Sie weiter und setzen Sie die korrekte Verbfom ein!

Usually, he **1.** let ___________ them ride, but today he **2.** want ___________ to close as quickly as possible and get to the pub. He takes a **broom** and starts to **sweep** the path.

Romeo and Juliet, he **3.** think ___________ to himself. Maybe **4.** it be ___________ Miss Whittam and Mr Thornton? Two of the boys' old drama teachers **recently** **5.** have ___________ an affair, and it **6.** be ___________ a scandal in the town. Peter remembers the **headline** in the local newspaper: "Real-life Romeo: Drama teacher brings family **shame**."

It's a bad choice of words anyway, Peter thinks. Romeo and Juliet ended up dead.

He picks up a crisp packet and a cola can and is walking towards the bin, when...

"Argh! Peter! Peter!"

"Peter!" comes the cry again. "Quick!"

All right, all right, Peter thinks. God, what's the big drama now? Why does Simon always...

"PETER!"

Something isn't right. Peter runs up the steps and into the station building. The clanking sound of the cable cars passing through the station has stopped, and the cars in the station are standing still. Simon is standing next to one. He is breathing heavily and his eyes are open wide with shock. The door to the car is open, and now Peter can see the girl inside. She is lying completely still. Her head is resting on the bar at the back of the cable car.

to reckon	meinen, vermuten
usually	normalerweise, gewöhnlich
broom	Besen
to sweep	kehren
recently	vor Kurzem
headline	Überschrift
shame	*hier*: Schande
choice of words	Wortwahl
to breathe heavily	schwer atmen
bar	*hier*: Stange
ambulance	Krankenwagen

"What's happened?" Peter asks. "Is she... She isn't...?"

Simon nods his head. "Yeah, she is. She's dead, Peter."

"Are you sure?"

"She's not breathing and she hasn't got a pulse. She's dead!"

"Where's the guy who came down with her?" Peter asks.

"I don't know!" Simon replies angrily. "She was on her own."

"We need to call the police and an ambulance."

"But what if..." Simon begins. "They might think we..."

"What? They might think we killed her? Don't be stupid!"

Simon doesn't answer. He just stands in silence.

Peter dials 999 and asks for the police. "…And we need an ambulance, too. At the lower cable car station in Happy Valley."

> 999 ist die Telefonnummer für jegliche Notfälle im Vereinigten Königreich. Als europaweite Alternative wurde 112 eingeführt.

Peter turns back and looks at his brother. He has turned white now, a lot whiter than the girl.

The girl has olive skin and long brown hair. She must be about 18 years old, Peter guesses. Far too young to die, surely? What happened? Why is there a beautiful dead girl in one of our cable cars?

"The police and an ambulance are on their way," Peter tells his brother when he has ended the call.

Exercise 3: Opposites. Finden Sie die Gegenteile im Text und schreiben Sie sie auf!

1. living ____________
2. lightly ____________
3. noise ____________
4. a long time ago ____________
5. too old ____________
6. to begin ____________

"What do we do now?" Simon asks slowly. "I've never found a dead body before…"

"And you think I'm an expert?" Peter snaps at his brother.

That's not fair, he then thinks. It really isn't Simon's fault she's dead. "I'm sorry, Simon," he says in a softer tone. "I think we should just wait here. Okay?"

Simon doesn't say anything. He just turns his back to Peter and stands in silence.

olive skin	olivfarbende Haut
to snap at sb.	jmd. anblaffen, anschnauzen
fault	Schuld

2 The Handbag

Detective Inspector Gareth Parry and Sergeant Rebecca Griffiths[i] from North Wales Police park their car and walk towards the lower cable car station in Happy Valley. It's colder now, but there are still a few people playing miniature golf and walking in the park. A group of children are buying ice cream from an ice cream van.

> Die Dienstgrade der britischen Polizei vom niedrigsten zum höchsten: Constable, Sergeant, Detective Inspector und Chief Inspector.

"It's the first time I've been here on duty, Gareth," Sergeant Griffiths tells her colleague in her high, young voice. "Happy Valley certainly isn't a crime hotspot."

"I know what you mean," DI Parry says and pushes open the gate to the station. "It's the side of Llandudno you see on postcards in souvenir shops."

DI Parry, a tall man in his late 40s with dark-rimmed glasses and a full head of grey hair, has worked on crimes across North Wales for years. But death in a cable car? This was a first. When the chief inspector told him about the unusual case, he asked Sergeant Griffiths to accompany him without a second thought. The 32-year-old sergeant is slim and petite, and

ice cream van	Eiswagen
on duty	im Dienst
voice	Stimme
crime hotspot	Zentrum des Verbrechens
dark-rimmed	dunkel umrandet
case	(Kriminal-)Fall
to accompany	begleiten
petite	zierlich

she appears younger than her years. Yet her professional pr
impressive, and Parry is sure she will be a high-flyer in the p
force.

Two male police officers and three other men are standing outside the entrance to the station building. Nobody is talking and Parry senses the awkward atmosphere immediately.

"Hello Inspector Parry, hello Sergeant Griffiths," one of the officers says. "I'm Sergeant Quinn and this is Sergeant Jones."

DI Parry and Sergeant Griffiths greet the officers. Parry then turns to the oldest of the three other men. He's around 50 years old and has a thick beard, old-fashioned glasses and a bad haircut.

"You must be Mr Cooper? You own the cable car, right?" he asks.

"That's right," Sergeant Quinn answers the question for Mr Cooper. "And the two young men are Peter and Simon Holland."

Peter and Simon look nervous. It is obvious they are brothers – they have the same large nose and red hair.

"Do the media know yet?" Mr Cooper asks. "I can see the headline in the papers now: 'Girl found dead on cable car.' It's going to be terrible for business."

to appear	*hier*: erscheinen
impressive	beeindruckend
high-flyer	Überflieger
to sense	spüren, wahrnehmen
to greet	begrüßen
beard	Bart
haircut	Frisur
obvious	offensichtlich
to investigate	untersuchen, ermitteln
to establish the facts	den Sachverhalt klären

"Mr Cooper," says Sergeant Griffiths, "please remember that we are here to investigate the death of a young girl. We need to establish the important facts and we need your help."

"DI Parry, would you and Sergeant Griffiths like to look inside?" asks Sergeant Quinn, and the group walk up the steps and into the station building.

Exercise 4: Translation. **Lesen Sie weiter und übersetzen Sie die deutschen Begriffe ins Englische!**

Inside, two pathologists are **examining** the **1.** jung __________ girl's body. They have taken it out of the cable car and **removed** some of her **2.** Kleider __________. Parry moves closer to look at her **3.** Gesicht __________. Her **4.** Augen __________ are closed, but he can see that she was very pretty. Pretty, but dead. All **signs** of life have already **disappeared** in the couple of **5.** Stunden __________ since her death. Her long brown **6.** Haar __________ is still shiny and thick, but her skin is now deathly pale.

The girl isn't an individual any more. She's a **piece of evidence**, an object for **scientific** examination.

"Hi, June," DI Parry says. "What can you tell us?"

"Hello, Gareth," says the pathologist June Crow. "Well, we don't know who the poor girl is. There was no handbag and no **purse**. But she's young. I'd say around 16. The

to examine	untersuchen
to remove	entfernen
sign	Zeichen
to disappear	verschwinden
piece of evidence	Beweisstück
scientific	wissenschaftlich
purse	Geldbeutel
paramedic	Sanitäter

paramedics were here, but she was already dead. The cable car workers say she was dead when they found her. That was at 5 p.m., not quite two hours ago. I'd say that sounds right. According to my quick examination, she has only been dead for a couple of hours."

"What is the probable cause of death?" Parry asks.

"We're not sure at the moment," Crow says. "There are no signs of violence, so we don't believe she was attacked."

probable	wahrscheinlich
violence	Gewalt

"According to Peter and Simon Holland, the girl arrived at the lower station alone," says Sergeant Quinn. "However, Peter says *two* people got into the cable car at the top."

Exercise 5: Word forms. **Ergänzen Sie das jeweilige Substantiv oder Verb!**

Noun	Verb
1. arrival	____________
2. ____________	to die
3. advice	____________
4. ____________	to examine

"That's what our colleague, Rhys, told us," says Peter. "He said 'Romeo and Juliet are coming down.' So I thought it was a couple. Boyfriend and girlfriend, you know?"

Sergeant Rebecca Griffiths turns to Peter. "So if there was a second person, a man, how did he get out? It's a cable car. If you get in at the top, surely you arrive at the bottom. It's too high to simply jump out."

"Not necessarily," says Mr Cooper, scratching his beard. "There is a point near the bottom where you could jump out. The cable car passes a cliff face. The cars are quite low at that point – only a couple of metres from some of the rocks. The cars don't have glass in the windows, as you can see. So you could jump out, theoretically."

He pauses then adds, "But I wouldn't advise it. You might break a bone or two. Only an idiot would jump out of a moving cable car."

"Or a criminal," says Sergeant Griffiths to DI Parry. "No teenage girl leaves the house without her handbag. So where is it? And her purse? Her mobile phone? Perhaps it was a robbery."

A robbery on a cable car?! That's absurd! DI Parry thinks, but he decides not to say anything. He doesn't want to discuss his own theories in front of the witnesses.

"Mr Holland," he says to Peter, "We'll need to talk to your colleague, Mr..."

not necessarily	nicht unbedingt
cliff face	Felswand
to advise	(be)raten
perhaps	vielleicht
robbery	Raubüberfall
witness	Zeuge/Zeugin
to swallow	schlucken
especially	besonders
to be about to do sth.	im Begriff sein, etw. zu tun
gloves *pl*	Handschuhe
to suffer from	leiden unter

"Matthews," says Peter. "Rhys Matthews."

"Thank you," says DI Parry.

He pushes his glasses further onto his nose and writes down the name in his notepad. "You two and Mr Matthews are important witnesses. We need your help to establish who this young girl is and what happened to her."

Simon, the younger brother, swallows hard. Peter no longer looks nervous, but Simon's face still looks white, especially against his bright red hair.

Why is he so terribly nervous? Parry asks himself. At that moment, his phone begins to ring.

"Yes, this is DI Parry."

"DI Parry," comes the voice at the other end. "This is Constable Tinker from Llandudno police station. I'm calling to inform you that somebody has handed in a handbag. It was found on the Great Orme earlier this evening."

"Her name is Rhiannon Thomas," DI Parry tells Sergeant Griffiths back in the car park.

"Do you think it's her?" Griffiths asks. "I mean, the handbag might belong to someone else."

"An officer is bringing the handbag now. There is a bus pass with a photo in the purse which we can use to identify her. But I already feel sure it's her. Tinker said the girl in the photo has long brown hair. Okay, a lot of girls have..." DI Parry stops when a police car drives into the car park. "**We're about to** find out."

A police officer gets out of the car and walks over to DI Parry and Sergeant Griffiths with a little brown handbag.

"Has anything been taken out?" Parry asks the officer.

"No," the officer replies. "It's all there."

The officer says goodbye and leaves Parry and Griffiths with the bag. Parry puts on a pair of latex **gloves** and takes the objects out of the bag. He looks at the photo.

"Yes, look. That's her."

Then he takes out a purse, a mobile phone, a bus ticket and, lastly, an inhaler.

"It looks like she **suffered from** asthma," Parry says, and hands the last object to his colleague.

"Possible cause of death?" Griffiths asks.

"Maybe. Up in a cable car, no inhaler. She panics and can't breathe. It would explain why there are no signs of violence."

Exercise 6: Unscramble the words. Lesen Sie weiter und bringen Sie die Buchstaben in die richtige Reihenfolge!

Parry takes the **1.** serup __________ and opens it. There are no credit or bank **2.** scadr __________ inside, but there is the **3.** sbu ssap __________ that Tinker **mentioned**. 'Rhiannon Thomas'. Parry recognizes the girl's face immediately. He sees her bright **4.** energ __________ eyes for the first time. The girl in the **5.** hoopt __________ has shorter hair than the dead girl, but it is clear they are the same **6.** sponer __________.

"It's her, isn't it?" says Griffiths.

Parry nods. "Yes. It's definitely her."

Parry then takes her touch-screen mobile phone.

"Two new messages," Parry tells Griffiths. "The first one is from someone called Cerys: 'So Rhi? How is it? Is he a good kisser? Don't do anything I wouldn't!' The second one is from her mother: 'Rhi, are you going to be home for dinner? love Mum.' There are two missed calls from her mother, too."

"No messages from a boy?" Griffiths asks.

"No *new* messages from a boy. But she did receive one at 11:04 from someone called Nick: 'Morning! Beautiful day! Looking forward to seeing you! See you on the pier at 3. Nick.'"

"Okay, so we need to find this 'Nick'."

"And speak to Rhys Matthews from the upper station. We need to know exactly who got into that cable car with the girl."
"And, Gareth," says Rebecca Griffiths, "we still have to contact the family and get them to identify the body."

to mention erwähnen

"Yes. We do." DI Parry looks at the phone in his hand again. Missed call: Mum.
He counts to five and then presses 'Call Mum' on the screen.
"Hello. Am I speaking to Mrs Thomas, Rhiannon's mother?" he asks. "Mrs Thomas, my name is Detective Inspector Gareth Parry from North Wales Police. I'm afraid I have some bad news."

3 The Instant Message

"It's 9:30. Here's a summary of the main news this morning from Radio Llandudno. The girl found dead in a cable car has been identified. The body of 15-year-old Rhiannon Thomas, who was a talented tennis player, was discovered yesterday afternoon by two attendants at the Happy Valley cable car station. Police are appealing for information from the public..."

Sergeant Rebecca Griffiths sighs and turns the bathroom radio off again. It was a typical news summary, just as she expected. Talented tennis player. Appeal for information. Nothing out of the ordinary. She walks down the stairs and back into the big, traditional kitchen.

summary	Zusammenfassung
to appeal	appellieren
to sigh	seufzen
nothing out of the ordinary	nichts Ungewöhnliches
opposite	gegenüber

"You found the bathroom?" Zoe Matthews asks.

"Yes, thank you, Mrs Matthews," Griffiths replies, and sits down at the antique kitchen table next to DI Parry and opposite 17-year-old Rhys Matthews and his mother, Zoe.

Rhys has a baby face but a well-built body. He is wearing a Wales rugby shirt, and DI Parry guesses he plays for a local team, like most teenage boys in the area.

"So Rhys, you say that this girl, Rhiannon Thomas, arrived at the upper cable car station at approximately five to five, and that she arrived with a man. Could you describe this man for us please?" DI Parry leans forward. "Tell us everything you remember, really everything."

Exercise 7: Synonyms. Finden Sie die Synonyme im Text und schreiben Sie sie auf!

1. adolescent ____________________
2. to answer ____________________
3. to not speak ____________________
4. to find ____________________
5. very old ____________________

to lean forward	sich nach vorn lehnen
ceiling	(Raum-)Decke
to tap	leicht klopfen
polite	höflich
to take notice of sb.	jmd. beachten

Rhys looks up at the ceiling and then down at the table. He is tapping his fingers on the table while he thinks.

"You said he was tall, my love, didn't you? I remember you said he was..." Zoe Matthews stops herself and pushes her styled blond hair behind her ears.

"Sorry," she says after a short pause. "I should keep quiet. You're interviewing Rhys, not me."

Parry gives her a small smile – a polite way of saying, 'Yes, that's right.'

"I don't really remember him that well. Just what my mum said, really. He was quite tall. A little older than me. Early 20s, maybe. But I didn't take much notice of him. He was just another customer."

"Why, then, did you describe the man and Rhiannon as 'Romeo and Juliet'?" DI Parry asks.

Exercise 8: Crossword puzzle. Lösen Sie das Kreuzworträtsel!

Across

4. nervös
6. Bemerkung
8. normal

Down

1. Eigenschaft
2. konzentrieren
3. nächster
5. der jüngere Holland-Bruder
7. einfarbig

Rhys continues tapping the table. "They were holding hands and kissing. They looked like... well, like they were deeply in love." He looks up at DI Parry. "It was just a joke. I mean, I know it wasn't funny. It was just a silly comment."

"Unfortunately, Inspector, Rhys is very good at making unfunny jokes," Zoe Matthews says. "And the Holland brothers aren't any better. If there's any trouble, Peter and Simon are usually not too far away."

"Don't say that, Mum!" Rhys throws his mother an angry look. "You barely know Peter and Simon. They're nice guys."

"Can we please concentrate on the man you saw with Rhiannon?" says DI Parry. "Every detail is important, Rhys. Even if it seems small to you. What colour was his hair? What was he wearing? Did he have any distinguishing features?"

barely	kaum
distinguishing feature	Unterscheidungsmerkmal
plain	*hier*: einfarbig
average	durchschnittlich
strange	seltsam, merkwürdig
to rule out	ausschließen

"He had brown hair, I think," Rhys says. "Errrm, I can't really remember what he was wearing. Maybe jeans and a plain T-shirt? And I don't think he had any distinguishing features. He was just... average-looking."

"And what happened next?"

"The couple got into a cable car and I sent them down. I called Peter to tell him the last couple for the day were coming down. I waited for Peter and Simon to stop the cars from the bottom station, and then I closed the upper station and drove home. When Peter called me to tell me what had happened, I couldn't believe it. I mean, it's just so strange. Do you think the guy killed her?"

Parry smiles and gives his standard reply.

"We're not ruling anything out at the moment."

Half an hour later, DI Parry and Sergeant Griffiths are moving slowly along the Llandudno seafront. Parry pushes his dark-rimmed glasses further onto his nose. Then he continues to tap his fingers on the **steering wheel**, frustrated at the slow-moving Sunday drivers.
Their interview with Rhys Matthews was **disappointing**. His description of the man with Rhiannon was poor and wouldn't be very useful at all.

steering wheel	Lenkrad
disappointing	enttäuschend
to confirm	bestätigen
wave	*hier*: ein Wink mit der Hand
useless	nutzlos
devastated	am Boden zerstört
to appreciate	wertschätzen

"Okay, thanks June," says Sergeant Griffiths, as she ends her phone call and turns to Parry. "The pathologists have **confirmed** that Rhiannon died of an asthma attack."
"Okay," Parry replies. "So we were right. She was having an asthma attack and needed her inhaler. But she was in the cable car and her inhaler was in her handbag on the ground below."
"Or the man had her handbag and wouldn't give it her."
"It's certainly possible..."
Ahead of them, a bus full of old ladies is parked at the side of the road. Parry stops to let a group of them cross the road. They smile and give a little **wave** to say 'thank you'.
"I'll try to ring the number for Nick again," Griffiths says.
She looks for Nick's number, which she took from the text message in Rhiannon's inbox: *Looking forward to seeing you! See you on the pier at 3. Nick*
Griffiths sighs. "Still no answer."
"Hopefully Rhiannon's friend Cerys Jenkins can help us. She knew about the date, so let's hope she knows Nick, too."
"I hope so. Rhiannon's parents certainly had no idea when we spoke to them last night. And Rhys Matthews' description of the man was **useless**. We won't get far with 'brown hair and average-looking'!"

Parry turns left into a side street, drives another hundred metres or so and then stops the car.

"Here we are. 41 St Michael's Road. Cerys Jenkins's house."
She looks **devastated**, thinks DI Parry when he sees Cerys in her family's back garden. She looks as if she has lost everything.
Cerys is wearing a big blue jumper and old jeans. She is sitting with her pet rabbit in her arms. The rabbit looks happy next to her warm body, but Cerys looks empty.

Exercise 9: Unscramble the text. Lesen Sie weiter und bringen Sie die Textabschnitte in die richtige Reihenfolge!

a) Sergeant Griffiths steps forward. "No, Cerys. We can stay here."

b) Cerys nods her head and then slowly asks, "Do we need to go to the police station?" She holds onto the rabbit tightly.

c) She lowers herself to look Cerys in the eye. "I know it's going to be very hard for you, but we really **appreciate** your help."

d) "Cerys, darling," her father says. "The police officers are here to speak to you. It's about Rhiannon. They need your help."

1	2	3	4

"She was my best friend. She was like my sister."
"Who did Rhiannon meet yesterday afternoon?" Griffiths asks.
Cerys puts down the rabbit and turns towards her.
"He was just this guy called Nick. I don't really know him. Did he do something to Rhi?"
"We don't know yet. We need to collect as much information as possible to find out. Do you know how Rhiannon met Nick?"
Now Cerys looks at her father and bites her lip.
"I'm sorry, Dad. I know I told you we stayed at Rhi's house last Saturday. But **actually**, we decided to go to the pub – The Horse and Hounds in Oak Street. Rhi said they never check how old you are. We just wanted to have a drink or two and have some fun. Are you angry, Dad?"
Mr Jenkins sighs. "Just tell the police officers the truth. That's the most important thing now."
"Nick started talking to Rhi and bought her a drink. I was **chatting** to another boy, so I didn't hear their conversation. I really don't know anything about him, **apart from** what he looked like."
Parry nods his head to **encourage** Cerys to continue.
"He looked quite a lot older than us. I'm not really sure how old. He was quite tall and had brown hair and designer stubble. Oh, and he had an eyebrow piercing. He was quite good-looking, I suppose. During the week, they made plans to meet on Saturday at 3 o'clock on the pier. I spoke to Rhi just before she met him. She was really excited. That's all I know really."
"So the last time you spoke to Rhiannon was shortly before 3 p.m. yesterday afternoon?"

actually	in der Tat, eigentlich
to chat	plaudern
apart from	außer
to encourage	ermuntern
upset	durcheinander, aufgebracht
⚡ bastard	Mistkerl, Schweinehund
to exaggerate	übertreiben
serious	ernst

Cerys begins to nod her head, but then she stops.
"Wait a minute. No. Actually, she sent me an instant message later in the day to see if I was online. I completely forgot about that. I was logged in, but... Oh my God, she said something about... I think she was upset! What did she tell me again?!"
"Have you still got this message?" Parry asks calmly.
"Errm, yes. I think so."
Cerys reaches for her phone and begins to look through her instant messages. She then hands the phone to Parry.
"That's it! That's what she said!"

Message from crazy_welsh_rhi at 16:41:
OMG, Cerys. He's an absolute bastard. Can't believe it. Want 2 talk 2 U now! R U there? Plz!

Exercise 10: Texting language. Schreiben Sie die typischen SMS- und Chatausdrücke in Standardenglisch auf!

1. OMG ____________________
2. Want 2 talk 2 U now ____________________
3. R U there? ____________________
4. Plz ____________________

Cerys starts to cry. "I thought she was just exaggerating! She does – I mean, she did that sometimes, and usually it wasn't serious. I was watching TV, so I ignored the message. And when I found out she was dead, I thought..."

Mr Jenkins sits down next to his daughter and **hugs** her.
"It's okay, darling. It's okay."
"I thought it was just her asthma. I didn't think about the message. I ignored her, Dad! I was too busy watching TV to care!"

to hug	umarmen
distracted	abgelenkt

DI Parry reads the message again. *An absolute bastard.*
"Sergeant Griffiths..." he begins, but his colleague is **distracted**. Her phone is ringing. She holds it up so that Parry can read the words on the screen: NICK CALLING.

4 Salad Days

Sergeant Griffiths walks to the end of the garden, away from Cerys and her father, and answers her phone.
"Hello?"

salad days *pl*	unschuldige Jugendjahre
line	*hier*: Leitung
ϟ slut	Schlampe
explanation	Erklärung
to assure	zusichern, vergewissern

She is surprised to hear a woman's voice at the other end of the **line**.
"You called my husband's phone five times this morning," the woman says angrily. "What do you want?"
"I called to talk to Nick. My name is Serge-"
"Nick?! Is that right? So you must be Rhiannon? Or are you another little **slut** who is texting *my* husband?" the woman demands. "And how old are you, anyway? You sound like a kid!"
"I think there's been a misunderstanding..."
"Listen to me. I've read the texts you sent. I need an **explanation**. Are you sleeping with my husband?"
"My name is Sergeant Rebecca Griffiths from North Wales Police, and I can **assure** you, madam, that I haven't sent *any* text messages to your husband. And I *certainly* haven't slept with him."
Silence. After a few seconds, the woman speaks.
"I'm sorry. I thought you... When you said 'Nick', you..."
"May I ask you your name, please, madam?"

DI Parry has turned to look at Griffiths. He looks a little alarmed. She makes an 'okay' sign with her right hand, so he turns back to Cerys. "Chantal Beale. This is my husband Hugh's phone..." the woman pauses.
Sergeant Griffiths can now hear a man's voice in the background, but she can't understand every word.

Exercise 11: Missing words. **Ergänzen Sie die Satzteile, die Sergeant Griffiths nicht hört!**

for a shower | problem | talking to | through my phone | on my phone

"Who are you **1.** __________? Why are you **2.** __________? Come here!... I go **3.** __________ and you start looking **4.** __________! What is your **5.** __________? Give it to me, now!"

"I've read the texts!" the woman shouts. "You told me I was paranoid, but I wasn't. Texts from someone called Rhiannon. 'It was great to meet you, too. Yes, that would be fun.' What would be fun, Hugh? A night with another woman while your wife and baby girl wait for you at home? You make me sick!"
"Just give me the phone, Chantal!"
After a few moments, the man comes onto the line.
"Hello, this is Hugh Beale. Who's calling?"
"My name is Sergeant Rebecca Griffiths. Actually, your wife called me, but I tried to ring you several times this morning. My colleague and I would like to speak to you, sir."

"Me? You want to speak to me? But I'm not sure how I can..."
"Let me rephrase that, sir. My colleague and I are going to speak to you, whether you like it or not. Now, please could you give me your address?"
Hugh Beale hesitates for a couple of seconds but then realizes he has no other option. Reluctantly, he gives her his address.
"Thank you, Mr Beale," says Griffiths. "We'll be with you shortly."

The young man who opens the door is tall and has brown hair and an eyebrow piercing. Bingo, thinks DI Parry.
"Mr Beale, I'm DI Parry." He holds up his identity card. "And this is Sergeant Griffiths. Can we come in, please?"
Chantal Beale is waiting in the living room. She has a very young baby in her arms. It must only be a couple of months old, thinks Parry. He isn't sure if Chantal looks angry or simply exhausted.
"Okay, will somebody please tell me what's going on?" she says. She has been crying, Parry thinks. She still has tears in her eyes.
"We are investigating the death of Rhiannon Thomas. Mr Beale, we believe you were with Miss Thomas yesterday afternoon."
Hugh Beale looks around the room like an animal trying to find a way out of a trap.
"What?" Chantal says, shocked. "You're investigating a death? What's this all about, Hugh?"
Beale's eyes settle on the coffee table. He can't look any of us in the eye, Parry thinks.
Five seconds of silence. Then Beale finally begins to speak.
"When I heard about it on the news, I felt sick. I didn't really know her. But I still felt sick. I met her at a bar last weekend. I told her my name was Nick, because I

to rephrase	umformulieren
to hesitate	zögern
reluctantly	ungern, wider-strebend
exhausted	erschöpft
trap	Falle
to feel sick	sich übel fühlen

didn't want her to know who I really was. She seemed interesting and witty. You and I, Chantal, we haven't really talked or laughed for so long. So it was just... refreshing. Then I suggested a date. I don't know why. I wasn't thinking straight. We met yesterday, on the pier, and then walked up the Great Orme. She suggested we get the cable car back down, and then... Chantal, why are you looking at me like that?"

Chantal has a look of horror on her face.

"The Great Orme cable car? It's that 15-year-old girl, isn't it? I saw it on the news this morning. Hugh, what have you done?"

"She was only 15?!" Hugh gasps. "Jesus Christ, I didn't..."

"What did you do to her, Hugh?" Chantal asks.

Hugh Beale waits for a second and slowly says, "I'm not going to say anything else now. I need to talk to a solicitor."

DI Parry nods at his colleague. "Okay, Sergeant Griffiths. Let's make use of that arrest warrant."

Exercise 12: True or false? Welche Aussagen sind korrekt? Markieren Sie mit richtig ✓ oder falsch – !

1. Chantal Beale comes to the door with her husband. ❒
2. Chantal Beale is surprised to hear that the officers are investigating a death. ❒
3. Hugh Beale says he met Rhiannon a week ago. ❒
4. Hugh Beale says he doesn't need a solicitor. ❒

A piece of a paper is stuck to the coffee machine at the North Wales Police headquarters in Colwyn Bay: OUT OF ORDER.

Brilliant, DI Parry thinks. I'll have to interview Beale without any caffeine in my body. Just brilliant.
"Everything okay, DI Parry?"
Parry turns to see the chief inspector, a large, round old man with a big red nose, walking towards him. "I hear you've made an arrest."

ϟ to think straight	logisch/klar denken
to gasp	vor Schreck hörbar einatmen
solicitor	Rechtsanwalt
arrest warrant	Haftbefehl
out of order	außer Betrieb
folder	Ordner

"That's right, sir."
"That was very quick indeed. Impressive. I knew you were the right man for the case. I'll speak to you after the interview."
"Okay, sir. Speak to you later."
"Ah! Constable Heaton!" the chief inspector shouts, and starts to walk towards an officer at the end of the corridor.
"Are you ready, Gareth?" says a voice behind DI Parry.
Parry turns to see Sergeant Griffiths. She is walking towards him with a folder full of documents in her hands.
Parry sighs. "Yes. I'm ready. I'm dying for a coffee, but I'm ready."

The two police officers head to the interview room together. Hugh Beale and his solicitor are already sitting at one side of a large table. The solicitor says something quietly to Beale – too quietly for Parry and Griffiths to hear.
Parry closes the door and sits down next to Griffiths.
"Mr Beale, where were you between 4:30 p.m. and 5:30 p.m. yesterday?"
"I've told you. I was with Rhiannon at first, on the Great Orme, but then I walked back down the hill and Rhiannon went somewhere else. And I never saw her again."
"So you're saying you weren't with Rhiannon when she arrived at the upper cable car station?"

"You heard him," says Beale's solicitor. "He walked down to the bottom. Rhiannon walked to the top."
"Your story has changed quite dramatically, Mr Beale," Sergeant Griffiths says. "Furthermore, you were a picture of guilt back at your house. But now you want me to believe that you calmly walked away from Rhiannon and never saw her again. You're not being very consistent, Mr Beale."

Exercise 13: Verbs. Lesen Sie weiter und unterstreichen Sie die passende Verbform!

"**1.** I'm telling / I tell the truth," Beale says. "I'm not proud of what I **2.** did / did do. I'm a married man and I went out with a young girl. A 15-year-old girl! I **3.** was thinking / thought she was older. She **4.** has told / told me she was 18! They all look so much older with their short dresses and their make-up. We flirted. We **5.** were / are alone. So I tried **6.** kiss / to kiss her, and..."

"Hugh, the police officers want to know about Rhiannon's death, not about your date," says the solicitor.
"Date? It sounds more like sexual assault to me!" comments Parry. "Okay, there was no rape. We know that. But you tried. You took her to the top of the Great Orme. Somewhere where nobody would hear her scream. She was scared. Hell, she was petrified! But she was only a child, and she didn't dare say no."

"No, no, no!" Beale shouts. "It wasn't like that. I stopped when I could see she was upset. She shouted at me. She called me a pervert, and then she *did* run away. She ran up the Great Orme, and I walked back down. I was angry with myself for being so... so stupid. I didn't want to scare her. I thought she *wanted* to have sex with me. She said she wanted to do 'adult things' with me. And I thought she was an adult!"

"No, Mr Beale. **Admit** it! You took her to the top of the Great Orme and put her in a cable car. You wanted to be high in the air, where no one could stop you. And when Rhiannon tried to get her phone out of her handbag and call for help, you **grabbed** her handbag and threw it out of the cable car."

"No! I didn't do any of this!"

"She panicked and had an asthma attack," Parry continues. "But her handbag had her inhaler in it, too. So she had nobody and nothing to save her. You made her panic, Mr Beale. You caused her asthma attack. Then the cable car passed by a cliff face and you jumped out. Admit it, Mr Beale!"

furthermore	darüber hinaus, des Weiteren
picture of guilt	Inbegriff der Schuld
consistent	konsequent, übereinstimmend
sexual assault	sexueller Übergriff
rape	Vergewaltigung
petrified	versteinert
to dare	es wagen, etw. zu tun
to admit	zugeben
to grab	etw. an sich reißen
to make sth. up	eine Geschichte erfinden

"DI Parry! I will not let you terrorize Mr Beale like this," shouts Beale's solicitor. "You are **making** this whole story **up**! Mr Beale may not be an angel, but he isn't a killer!"

The solicitor is looking Parry straight in the eye. "Mr Beale isn't a killer. And you know it."

For a moment, the room is silent. Then Hugh Beale begins to cry.

Exercise 14: Match up the phrases. Verbinden Sie die Begriffe!

1.	☐ look someone	a)	for help
2.	☐ run	b)	in the eye
3.	☐ call	c)	a story
4.	☐ make up	d)	away

5 Key Evidence

"I'm sorry, June!" says DI Parry when he arrives at the lower cable car station an hour later. "I was interviewing Hugh Beale. I came as soon as I received your message about the key."

"That's okay," June Crow replies. "Where's Sergeant Griffiths?"

"She's organizing an **identity parade**. We need Rhys Matthews to identify Hugh Beale as the man who got into the cable car with Rhiannon. But tell me all about the key the **forensic** team found."

"This is it," Crow says, handing Parry a plastic **wallet** with a little silver key inside.

Parry holds it up to his eyes. The key has two large teeth and two small teeth. Like a little, square, euro sign, Parry thinks.

"We found it there," Crow continues, and points to the cliff.

identity parade	Gegenüberstellung
forensic	gerichtsmedizinisch
wallet	*hier*: Mappe
remote	abgelegen
steep	steil

They have a good view of the Great Orme cliff from the station.

"It was about halfway down, behind those trees, to the left of the cable car. It's a **remote** area. Too **steep** for footpaths."

"So the key didn't belong to a walker. And it probably wasn't dropped from a cable car," Parry says. "It's too far away, isn't it?"

"Exactly. We found it about 80 metres south of the cable car line. What's more, the key was clean when we found it. And it was on top of the vegetation. So however it got there, it got there recently. Certainly after Thursday's heavy rain."

Parry's eyes follow the cable car line out of the station, up the cliff and into the distance. It is quite dark now. Storm clouds are forming in the sky. The still, empty cable cars now appear unwelcoming, even dangerous.

"So if you can prove the key belongs to Hugh Beale," Crow says, "you'll have a good case against him. My theory is this: Beale jumps out of the cable car, onto the cliff, and tries to get away and down to the bottom as quickly as possible. But he's on very steep ground. He has to do a lot of jumping and climbing, and a key falls out of his pocket. But he doesn't notice. He continues home."

It's quite possible, Parry thinks. And we don't have another theory at the moment. It certainly makes sense...

Exercise 15: Odd one out. Welches Wort ist das „schwarze Schaf"? Unterstreichen Sie!

1. sometimes possible probable likely
2. rainy cloudy sunny stormy
3. plastic metal pocket paper
4. climb jump think walk

Parry's mobile interrupts his thoughts.

"Yes, this is DI Parry."

"Hello Inspector. Sergeant Quinn from Llandudno police here. I'm calling with information on the Rhiannon Thomas case. A witness has come forward."

DI Parry listens intently.

"A local woman, 50 years old. She was walking her dogs on the Great Orme yesterday afternoon and saw an argument between a young woman and a man. Her description fits Rhiannon and Hugh Beale. She says she watched them from a distance. After a few minutes, they separated: the girl went uphill, the man downhill."

What?! thinks Parry. Rhiannon went to the top alone?

For a moment, he is speechless. This changes everything, he thinks. Beale has an alibi. He isn't Romeo...

"And she's a trustworthy witness," Quinn says. "There's no connection between her and Beale."

DI Parry jumps when suddenly someone knocks at the door. He turns round and the door slowly opens. A nervous Mr Cooper, the cable car owner, appears. 'Sorry!' he silently mouths to Parry and Crow.

"Sergeant Quinn, I'll ring you back in five minutes." Parry ends the call. "Mr Cooper, can we help you?"

"I'm sorry, DI Parry," he says. "But I forgot that the week's takings are still in the safe. With all the drama yesterday, I forgot to take them home with me."

"Of course," Parry says. "But I'll have to watch you, Mr Cooper. Remember this is a crime scene."

"I certainly haven't forgotten, Inspector," Cooper says sarcastically. "Closing my station for your investigations is losing me quite a lot of money, you know."

In the office, Mr Cooper takes his keys out of his pocket. There are about seven or eight keys on the chain. Two small, silver keys catch Parry's attention.

unwelcoming	nicht einladend, unwirtlich
to interrupt	unterbrechen
to come forward	sich (bei der Polizei) melden
intently	hoch konzentriert, aufmerksam
trustworthy	vertrauenswürdig
to mouth	Worte lautlos sagen
takings *pl*	Einnahmen
chain	Kette
to catch sb.'s attention	jds. Aufmerksamkeit erregen

"May I quickly look at that key chain, Mr Cooper?" Parry asks. Cooper, a little **confused**, hands Parry the keys. Parry recognizes the 'square euro sign' teeth of one key immediately.
"What is this key for, Mr Cooper?" he asks.
"That's... errrm... the upper station key. Why?" Cooper looks even more confused.
"And how many copies are there of this key?" Parry continues. "Do your workers have a copy each?"

confused	verwirrt
to lock up	abschließen
ϟ He wouldn't hurt a fly.	Er würde keiner Fliege etw. zu Leide tun.
convincing	überzeugend
to wonder	sich fragen
prime suspect	Hauptverdächtiger
to whisper	flüstern

"Well, not all of them. Only Rhys. Simon and Peter have a copy of the lower station key, this one here." He points at the second small key.
"And may I ask, Mr Cooper, does Rhys always drive home after he has **locked up**? Or might he, theoretically, lock the station from the *inside* and take the cable car down to Happy Valley?"
Mr Cooper doesn't say anything for a few seconds. He now understands what Parry is suggesting. And Parry can see his shock. *Rhys*? his eyes seem to say. *You think it was Rhys?*
"Well, I... He sometimes comes down in the cable car. But not yesterday. He said he drove down yesterday."
Mr Cooper studies the detective's face for a second and then says, "DI Parry, Rhys **wouldn't hurt a fly**. No way."
But his voice is not really **convincing**.
Who is he trying to convince? DI Parry **wonders**. Me or himself?
"Honestly, I really don't think..." Mr Cooper begins.
But it is useless. He, too, is starting to see the cable car worker in a very different light.
"Excuse me," Parry says. "I have a suspect to interview."

Exercise 16: Prepositions. **Lesen Sie weiter und ergänzen Sie die fehlenden Präpositionen!**

at | on | over | to | with

DI Parry and Sergeant Griffiths arrive **1.** ______ Rhys Matthews' house together. Sergeant Griffiths has already discussed the possible identity parade **2.** ______ Rhys **3.** ______ the phone, and Zoe Matthews is surprised **4.** ______ see the officers back **5.** ______ her doorstep again that day.

"Officers. Isn't it a little late?" she asks.
Indeed, the stormy late afternoon has turned into a stormy evening, and Parry would normally wait until the next morning to interview a witness for the second time.
But Rhys is no longer just a witness. He's the **prime suspect**.
"I'm sorry, Mrs Matthews," Parry answers. "But it really is very important."
Zoe Matthews sighs. "Come in, then. Rhys is in his bedroom. I'll just go and get him. Please take a seat."
"As I said before," Griffiths **whispers** to Parry, when Zoe Matthews has left the room, "Rhys didn't like the idea of an identity parade when I spoke to him on the phone. He said he'd completely forgotten what Romeo looked like."
Parry smiles. "I don't believe that for a second. I reckon Rhys never stops looking in the mirror."

Rhys looks exhausted when he walks into the kitchen. There are lines around his eyes. As if he has **aged** over the past ten hours.
"Good evening, Rhys," says Parry. "Now, **let's get down to business**, shall we? You lied to me and Sergeant Griffiths this morning. Rhiannon arrived at the cable car station alone. That's not a question, but a fact. So, if Juliet arrived at the upper station alone, Rhys... there is only one person who could be Romeo."
"But, erm, no she was with... maybe he was... erm..."
"This is yours, isn't it?" Parry takes out the key. "Rhys?"
"I've no idea... I, honestly, I..."
Zoe Matthews takes her son's hand. "Honey, you don't have to answer these questions. Not without a solicitor. Because you didn't do anything, did you?"

to age	altern
Let's get down to business.	Kommen wir zur Sache.
to cheer sb. up	jmd. aufmuntern
to rock	schaukeln
to pretend	tun als ob
to arrest sb.	jmd. verhaften

Rhys turns to his mother, and tears begin to appear in his eyes.
"It was just a... Just a joke, Mum. I wanted to **cheer her up** and make her laugh. I **rocked** the cable car a little bit. But she didn't find it funny. I **pretended** to look in her handbag, just because... I don't know why any more! I was just flirting! Usually girls like it when I flirt. They know it's just a joke, but she..."
Sergeant Griffiths is about to ask a question, but Parry taps the table quietly to say 'Let's just listen.'
"...She tried to grab her bag back from me... I could see she was upset, but... Suddenly, she couldn't breathe, and... I don't know any more. I panicked and threw the bag at her and she pushed me away at the same time. The bag fell out of the window. And then *she* really panicked. She couldn't breathe, and she just kept saying 'My inhaler! My inhaler!' Again and again, until..."
Rhys pauses. "I didn't want her to die. But it was too late. She was already dead. I couldn't save her. So I jumped out."

He hangs his head in shame. "I jumped out and left her there."
"Why didn't you just tell the truth?" Zoe Matthews asks her son slowly. "Why didn't you tell me this before, Rhys?"
Sergeant Griffiths turns to DI Parry and he nods. This time, Parry knows they are **arresting** the right Romeo.

Exercise 17: Where does that happen? Beantworten Sie die Fragen und enträtseln Sie das Lösungswort!

1. In which building does DI Parry see the chief inspector?
2. In which town does the story take place?
3. Where do Rhiannon and Hugh Beale go walking together?
4. In chapter 3, in which room do DI Parry and Sergeant Griffiths interview Rhys Matthews?
5. In which room does Sergeant Griffiths hear the news on the radio?

1. _ _ _ _ _ _   _ _ _ _ _ _ □
2. _ _ _ _ _ _ _ _ □
3. _ □ _ _ _   _ _ _ _
4. _ _ □ _ _ _ _
5. _ _ _ □ _ _ _ _

Lösung: The story takes place in a town in _ _ _ _ _ Wales.

Final Test

Answers

Glossary

List of Exercises

Final Test

Exercise 1: Acronyms. Wofür stehen die folgenden Abkürzungen! Schreiben Sie auf!

1. CEO ______________________

2. IT ______________________

3. MP ______________________

Exercise 2: Business crossword puzzle. Setzen Sie die Begriffe zum Thema „Business“ ein.

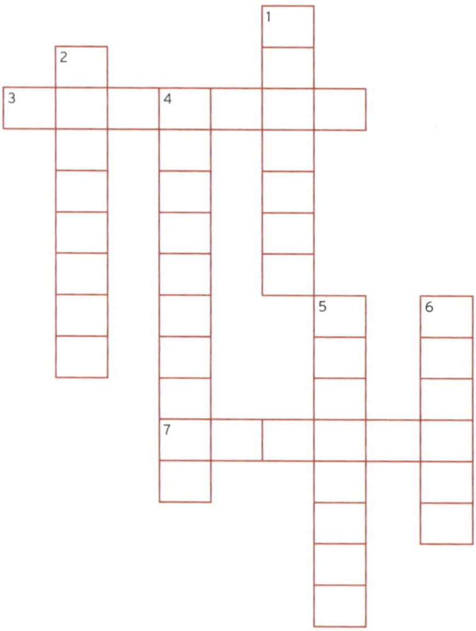

Across

3. Firma

7. Büro

Down

1. Finanzen

2. Auftrag

4. Produktion

5. Ehrgeiz

6. Karriere

Exercise 3: Places translation. Übersetzen Sie die Begriffe für Orte ins Englische!

1. U-Bahnhof ______________________
2. Kindergarten ______________________
3. Wolkenkratzer ______________________
4. Volkshochschule ______________________

Exercise 4: Hidden words. Finden Sie die 11 versteckten Wörter, die mit Polizeiarbeit zu tun haben!

O	A	U	T	O	P	S	Y	K	I	M	A
T	L	W	E	I	L	P	H	L	C	O	J
R	I	N	V	E	S	T	I	G	A	T	E
M	B	J	I	B	N	C	Y	L	L	E	O
A	I	M	C	H	G	M	O	T	I	V	E
C	P	S	T	R	S	A	T	I	R	H	W
R	E	U	I	A	V	O	W	F	O	J	I
I	R	S	M	U	R	D	E	R	R	W	T
M	C	P	U	X	U	D	A	D	Y	C	N
E	N	E	M	I	E	S	P	I	M	A	E
J	V	C	T	M	K	B	O	P	C	L	S
O	U	T	P	L	E	Y	N	I	E	B	S

Exercise 5: Odd one out. Welches Wort ist das „schwarze Schaf“? Unterstreichen Sie!

1. personal assistant | employer | staff member | employee
2. dagger | paper knife | scalpel | gun
3. suddenly | at once | immediately | now
4. to sack | to let go | to retire | to fire

Exercise 6: Verb forms. Ergänzen Sie die fehlenden Verbformen!

	Infinitive	Present Participle	Past Simple
1.	scream	____________	____________
2.	____________	____________	drove
3.	____________	going	____________
4.	____________	____________	was/were
5.	do	____________	____________
6.	____________	seeing	____________
7.	take	____________	____________
8.	____________	____________	hurt
9.	____________	keeping	____________

Exercise 7: Questions to the text. Beantworten Sie die Fragen zu „Guided Murder“!

1. Who is Petra Berkl?

____

2. What is Kyle Simmons' job?

____

3. Which attractions do the tourists visit in London?

____

4. What happens to Sheila at the end of the story?

____

Exercise 8: Non-standard English. Verbinden Sie die umgangssprachlichen Begriffe mit den Standardbegriffen.

1. ☐ fit	a) stupid
2. ☐ slow	b) child
3. ☐ guy	c) attractive
4. ☐ bastard	d) man
5. ☐ kid	e) a bad man

Exercise 9: Conjunctions. **Ergänzen Sie die fehlenden Bindewörter!**

although | and | because | but | if | however | when

It's shortly before 5 o'clock **1.** ______ Rhiannon arrives at the upper cable car station. She goes inside **2.** ______ sees a young man working there.

"Can I help you, darling?" Rhys asks, smiling at her as friendly as possible.

"I just want to go down to Llandudno, **3.** ______ that's okay?" she asks.

"Of course! **4.** ______, there's one condition. **5.** ______ you've got such a pretty face, I'd like to come down with you."

Rhiannon just wants to be alone, **6.** ______ what can she do – she has to take the cable car.

"Okay," she says, **7.** ______ she is not happy. "Just get me to the bottom."

They both climb inside.

"Just relax," Rhys says.

Exercise 10: Idioms. Verbinden Sie die Satzteile zu idiomatischen Ausdrücken!

1. ☐ We can't	a) think straight.
2. ☐ I tried to catch	b) a drink.
3. ☐ He wouldn't hurt	c) rule it out.
4. ☐ I couldn't	d) a fly.
5. ☐ She's dying for	e) his attention.
6. ☐ He's keeping	f) before they're hatched.
7. ☐ I think I touched	g) an eye on her.
8. ☐ It's neck	h) a nerve.
9. ☐ Don't count your chickens	i) and neck.

Exercise 11: Definitions. Schreiben Sie das beschriebene Wort auf!

1. legal representative ____________
2. statement of truth ____________
3. a line of waiting people ____________
4. what you keep your money in ____________
5. the room where you work ____________

Answers

Deadly Business

Exercise 1: **1.** c **2.** a **3.** d **4.** b

Exercise 2: **1.** out of **2.** towards **3.** to **4.** along **5.** on **6.** with

Exercise 3: **1.** d **2.** a **3.** b **4.** c

Exercise 4: **1.** handsome **2.** door **3.** body **4.** thick **5.** eyes **6.** information

Exercise 5:

1 R	2 O	3 T	4 H	5 A	6 N
20 A	21 L	22 T	23 H	24 O	7 D
19 E	32 M	33 A	34 I	25 T	8 E
18 H	31 E	36 S	35 L	26 E	9 E
17 T	30 G	29 R	28 A	27 L	10 P
16 U	15 R	14 T	13 N	12 A	11 L

Exercise 6: **1.** b **2.** d **3.** c **4.** a

Exercise 7: **1.** mobile **2.** power **3.** guilty **4.** surprise

Exercise 8: **1.** b **2.** c **3.** a **4.** d

Exercise 9: **1.** lights **2.** dark **3.** skirt **4.** spying **5.** surprised **6.** smoking

Exercise 10: **1.** He can see skyscrapers.
2. He feels sick because of the stress/because he is so stressed.
3. She is angry because he forgot to fill up the car with petrol.
4. He ends the call by throwing his mobile phone across his desk.

Exercise 11: **1.** told **2.** went **3.** weren't (nicht 'wasn't') **4.** don't know **5.** there's

Exercise 12: **1.** It's neck and neck.
2. He is keeping an eye on her.
3. I think I touched a nerve.
4. Don't count your chickens before they're hatched.

Exercise 13: **1.** true **2.** false (He is pretending to read a newspaper.) **3.** true **4.** false (A couple of her best friends know.)

Exercise 14: **1.** follow **2.** suspicious **3.** voice **4.** impatient **5.** late

Exercise 15: **1.** a **2.** b **3.** a **4.** c

Exercise 16: **1.** d **2.** c **3.** a **4.** b

Exercise 17: **1.** know **2.** had **3.** to **4.** your **5.** life **6.** didn't

Guided Murder

Exercise 1: **1.** office **2.** view **3.** boss **4.** chair **5.** think **6.** mood

Exercise 2: **1.** doesn't **2.** they're **3.** I'm **4.** She'll

Exercise 3: **1.** c **2.** d **3.** a **4.** b

Exercise 4: **1.** you **2.** us **3.** our **4.** me **5.** myself **6.** my

Exercise 5: **1.** cold **2.** sadly **3.** horrible **4.** dark **5.** empty **6.** open

Exercise 6: **1.** wanted **2.** said **3.** did **4.** had **5.** stood

Exercise 7: **1.** when **2.** Where **3.** What **4.** Why

Exercise 8: **1.** up **2.** with **3.** towards **4.** at **5.** outside **6.** on

Exercise 9: **1.** does **2.** is **3.** finished **4.** gone **5.** sitting **6.** resting

Exercise 10: **1.** statement **2.** wound **3.** enemies **4.** expression **5.** imagine **6.** scared **7.** exhausted
Lösung: suspect

Exercise 11: **1.** c **2.** a **3.** b **4.** d

Exercise 12: **1.** elegant **2.** politely **3.** strangely **4.** exclusive **5.** important

Exercise 13: **1.** myself **2.** want **3.** answers **4.** says **5.** too **6.** was

Exercise 14: **1.** true **2.** false, a cosy pub **3.** false, They are wearing plainclothes. **4.** false, He had money problems and gambling debts.

Exercise 15: **1.** c **2.** a **3.** d **4.** b

Exercise 16: **1.** forgot **2.** heard **3.** speaking **4.** talk **5.** called **6.** having **7.** punches

Exercise 17: **1.** right hand **2.** drawer **3.** doesn't see it **4.** dead **5.** finally

Breathlessly Beautiful

Exercise 1: **1.** c **2.** a **3.** d **4.** b

Exercise 2: **1.** would let **2.** wants **3.** thinks **4.** it's **5.** had **6.** was

Exercise 3: **1.** dead **2.** heavily **3.** silence **4.** recently **5.** too young **6.** to end

Exercise 4: **1.** young **2.** clothes **3.** face **4.** eyes **5.** hours **6.** hair

Exercise 5: **1.** arrive **2.** death **3.** advise **4.** examination

Exercise 6: **1.** purse **2.** cards **3.** bus pass **4.** green **5.** photo **6.** person

Exercise 7: **1.** teenager **2.** to reply **3.** to keep quiet **4.** to discover **5.** antique

Exercise 8:

	1 F			2 C						3 N
4 N	E	R	V	O	U	5 S				E
	A			N		I				X
	T			6 C	O	M	M	E	N	T
	U			E		O				
	R			N		N				
	E			T			7 P			
				R			L			
		8 S	T	A	N	D	A	R	D	
				T			I			
				E			N			

Exercise 9: **1.** d **2.** b **3.** a **4.** c

Exercise 10: **1.** Oh my God. **2.** I want to talk to you now. **3.** Are you there? **4.** Please.

Exercise 11: **1.** talking to **2.** on my phone **3.** for a shower **4.** through my phone **5.** problem

Exercise 12: **1.** false **2.** true **3.** true **4.** false

Exercise 13: **1.** I'm telling **2.** did **3.** thought **4.** told **5.** were **6.** to kiss

Exercise 14: **1.** b **2.** d 3 a **4.** c

Exercise 15: **1.** sometimes **2.** sunny **3.** pocket **4.** think

Exercise 16: **1.** at **2.** with **3.** over **4.** to **5.** on

Exercise 17: **1.** police station **2.** Llandudno **3.** Great Orme **4.** kitchen **5.** bathroom
Lösung: North

Final Test

Exercise 1: **1.** Chief Executive Officer **2.** Information Technology **3.** Member of Parliament

Exercise 2:

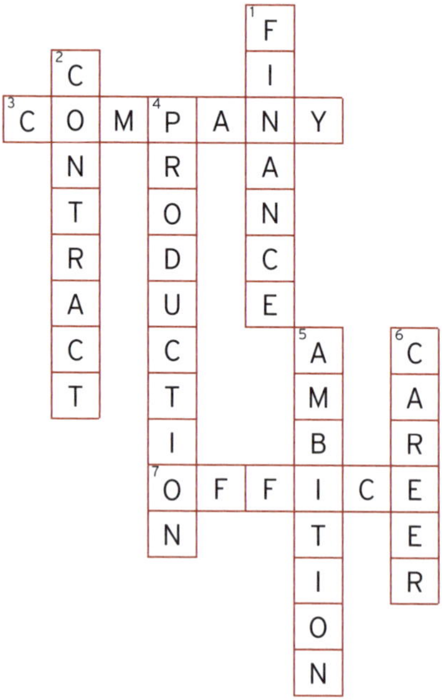

Exercise 3: **1.** underground station **2.** nursery **3.** skyscraper **4.** community college

Exercise 4:

O	A	U	T	O	P	S	Y	K	I	M	A
T	L	W	E	I	L	P	H	L	C	O	J
R	I	N	V	E	S	T	I	G	A	T	E
M	B	J	I	B	N	C	Y	L	L	E	O
A	I	M	C	H	G	M	O	T	I	V	E
C	P	S	T	R	S	A	T	I	R	H	W
R	E	U	I	A	V	O	W	F	O	J	I
I	R	S	M	U	R	D	E	R	R	W	T
M	C	P	U	X	U	D	A	D	Y	C	N
E	N	E	M	I	E	S	P	I	M	A	E
J	V	C	T	M	K	B	O	P	C	L	S
O	U	T	P	L	E	Y	N	I	E	B	S

Exercise 5: **1.** employer **2.** gun **3.** suddenly **4.** to retire

Exercise 6: **1.** screaming, screamed **2.** drive, driving **3.** go, went **4.** be, being **5.** doing, did **6.** see, saw **7.** taking, took **8.** hurting, hurt **9.** keep, kept

Exercise 7: **1.** Petra Berkl is a German tourist visiting London. She works as a homicide detective in Berlin.
2. Kyle Simmons owns a casino.
3. The tourists visit the British Museum, Armstrong House and Westminster Abbey. They also go to see a musical.
4. Sheila dies after she shoots herself with her own gun.

Exercise 8: **1.** c **2.** a **3.** d **4.** e **5.** b

Exercise 9: **1.** when **2.** and **3.** if **4.** However **5.** Because **6.** but **7.** although

Exercise 10: **1.** c **2.** e **3.** d **4.** a **5.** b **6.** g **7.** h **8.** i **9.** f

Exercise 11: **1.** solicitor **2.** fact **3.** queue **4.** purse **5.** office

Glossary

ϟ = umgangssprachlich
pl = Plural

to accompany	begleiten
actually	in der Tat, eigentlich
to admit	zugeben
ϟ adult stuff	*hier*: erwachsene Themen
to advise	(be)raten
aging	alternd
to age	altern
ambulance	Krankenwagen
anger	Zorn
annoyance	Verärgerung
annoyed	genervt
apart from	außer
to appeal	appellieren
to appear	sich zeigen, auftauchen; erscheinen
appointment	Termin
to appreciate	wertschätzen
to arrest sb.	jmd. verhaften
arrest warrant	Haftbefehl
Assistant Manager	Direktionsassistent(in)
to assure	zusichern, vergewissern
at once	sofort, gleich
attendant	Aufseher(in)

attentively	aufmerksam
available	zur Verfügung stehen
average	durchschnittlich
awful	schrecklich
awkward	verlegen, peinlich
badge	*hier*: Dienstmarke
bar	*hier*: Stange
barely	kaum
ϟ bastard	Mistkerl, Schweinehund
to be able to afford sth.	sich etw. leisten können
to be about to do sth.	im Begriff sein, etw. zu tun
to be against the rules	gegen die Regeln verstoßen
beanie	(Beanie-)Mütze
to bear a grudge	einen Groll hegen
beard	Bart
to bear to do sth.	es ertragen, etw. zu tun
to be fooled	hereingelegt, getäuscht
to be in the mood for sth.	Lust haben auf etw.
to be on first name terms	per du sein
to be tempted	versucht sein
blackmail	Erpressung
to blackmail	erpressen
blame	Schuld
to blame sb.	jmd. die Schuld geben
blankly	ausdruckslos
to blink	blinzeln
ϟ Bloody hell!	Verdammt!
break	*hier*: Lücke; Pause
to breathe a sigh of relief	erleichtert aufatmen
to breathe heavily	schwer atmen
to bribe	bestechen
briefcase	Aktentasche/-koffer

broom	Besen
bun	*hier*: Dutt
button	Knopf
by mistake	aus Versehen
cable car	Seilbahn
to call in sick	sich krank melden
car horn	Autohupe
case	(Kriminal-)Fall
to catch sb.'s attention	jds. Aufmerksamkeit erregen
ceiling	(Raum-)Decke
chain	Kette
change	Wechselgeld
to change one's mind	seine Meinung ändern
to change the subject	das Thema wechseln
to chat	plaudern
to cheer sb. up	jmd. aufmuntern
chest	Brust(korb)
chief executive officer (CEO)	Geschäftsführer(in)
choice of words	Wortwahl
cliff face	Felswand
closing time	Feierabend
clue	Hinweis, Anhaltspunkt
to come forward	sich (bei der Polizei) melden
to come to an agreement	sich einigen
to compare	vergleichen
to compete	*hier*: kämpfen
competitor	Konkurrent
condition	Bedingung
to confirm	bestätigen
confused	verwirrt
connected	verbunden
consistent	konsequent, übereinstimmend

contract	*hier*: Auftrag
to contrast with	*hier*: ergänzen
convinced	überzeugt
convincing	überzeugend
cosy	gemütlich
counter	Tresen, Theke
crime hotspot	Zentrum des Verbrechens
ϟ crooked	unehrlich
crucial	entscheidend
curiosity	Neugier
dagger	Dolch
to dare	es wagen, etw. zu tun
dark-rimmed	dunkel umrandet
debts *pl*	Schulden
decade	Jahrzehnt
to depend	von etw. abhängen
designer stubble	Dreitagebart
determined	entschlossen
devastated	am Boden zerstört
development	Entwicklung
to disappear	verschwinden
disappointing	enttäuschend
disbelief	Unglaube
disgusted	empört
distinguishing feature	Unterscheidungsmerkmal
distracted	abgelenkt
to disturb sb.	jmd. stören
to donate	spenden
doorframe	Türrahmen
dot	Punkt
doubt	Zweifel
drive	Auffahrt

to elect	wählen
emergency	Notfall
emphasis	Betonung
employee	Angestellte(r)
to encourage	ermuntern
enemy	Feind(in)
equal	*hier*: gleichwertig
to escape	entkommen
especially	besonders
to establish the facts	den Sachverhalt klären
evening dress	Abendkleidung
to exaggerate	übertreiben
to examine	untersuchen
exhausted	erschöpft
exhausting	sehr anstrengend
explanation	Erklärung
expression	Ausdruck
eyebrow	Augenbraue
factory	Fabrik
ϟ to fancy	Lust haben auf
ϟ fat cat	Bonze
fault	Schuld
to feel one's blood boil	kochen vor Wut
to feel sick	sich übel fühlen
felt-tip pen	Filzstift
fiancé/fiancée	Verlobter/Verlobte
to fire sb.	feuern, jmd. entlassen
ϟ fit	sexy, attraktiv
flat	Wohnung
flirtatiously	kokett
folder	Ordner
to follow sth. up	etw. nachverfolgen

for good	endgültig
forensic	gerichtsmedizinisch
foul play	Verbrechen
to frown	die Stirn runzeln
furious	wütend, bitterböse
furthermore	darüber hinaus, des Weiteren
to gamble	um Geld spielen
to gasp	vor Schreck hörbar einatmen
to get lucky	Glück/Erfolg haben
to give sb. notice	vorwarnen
gloves *pl*	Handschuhe
good cop/bad cop	guter Bulle/böser Bulle
ϟ gossip mag	Klatschmagazin
to grab	etw. an sich reißen
to grant	erteilen, gewähren
to greet	begrüßen
guided tour	Führung
guilty	schuldig
haircut	Frisur
hallway	Flur
handcuffs *pl*	Handschellen
handsome	gut aussehend
to have a heart-to-heart	ein ernstes Gespräch haben
headline	Überschrift
to hesitate	zögern
ϟ He wouldn't hurt a fly.	Er würde keiner Fliege etw. zu Leide tun.
high-flyer	Überflieger
to hiss	fauchen
homicide	Mord
horrible	schrecklich, grausam
hospital ward	Krankenstation

How dare you!	Was erlauben Sie sich!, Was fällt dir ein!
to hug	umarmen
to hurry	sich beeilen
to hurt sb.	jmd. weh tun
to introduce sb.	jmd. vorstellen, bekanntmachen
ice cream van	Eiswagen
identity parade	Gegenüberstellung
to imagine sth.	sich etw. vorstellen
impatient(ly)	ungeduldig
impressive	beeindruckend
in any case	wie dem auch sei
information technology	Informationstechnik
inheritance	Erbe
injured	verletzt
intently	hoch konzentriert, aufmerksam
to interrupt	unterbrechen
to investigate	untersuchen, ermitteln
to keep an eye on sb./sth.	jmd./etw. im Auge behalten
to keep sb.	jmd. aufhalten
late	*hier*: verstorben
law	Gesetz
lawyer	Anwalt
lead	(heiße) Spur
to lean	sich lehnen
to lean across	sich herüber beugen
to lean forward	sich nach vorn lehnen
to let sb. go	*hier*: jmd. entlassen, feuern
Let's get down to business.	Kommen wir zur Sache.
library	Bibliothek
line	*hier*: Leitung
ϟ liquid lunch	Alkohol statt Mittagessen

to lock up	abschließen
to loosen	lockern
to lose	verlieren
to lose one's temper	die Beherrschung verlieren
ϟ lot	*hier*: Haufen, Pack
to make sth. up	eine Geschichte erfinden
mature	reif
Memorial Fountain	Gedenkbrunnen
to mention	erwähnen
mid-sentence	mitten im Satz
Mind the step!	Vorsicht Stufe!
moustache	Schnurrbart
to mouth	Worte lautlos sagen
MP (Member of Parliament)	Abgeordnete(r)
ϟ My money is on ...	*hier*: Ich tippe auf ...
nastily	fies, gemein
never mind	Schon gut!, Vergiss es!
to nod	nicken
none of your business	das geht dich nichts an
to not give a damn about sth.	auf etw. pfeifen
to not have a clue	keine Ahnung haben
not necessarily	nicht unbedingt
nothing out of the ordinary	nichts Ungewöhnliches
number plate	Autokennzeichen
nursery	Kindergarten
obvious	offensichtlich
to offer	anbieten
olive skin	olivfarbende Haut
on duty	im Dienst
one-on-one	Einzel...
(golden) opportunity	(einmalige) Gelegenheit
opposite	Gegenteil; gegenüber

order	Befehl
otherwise	sonst
out of order	außer Betrieb
pair of binoculars	Fernglas
paper knife	Brieföffner
paramedic	Sanitäter
pathetic	erbärmlich, jämmerlich, armselig
perhaps	vielleicht
permission	Zulassung
petite	zierlich
petrified	versteinert
picture of guilt	Inbegriff der Schuld
piece of evidence	Beweisstück
pint	*hier*: ein Bier (ca. 0,56 l)
plain	*hier*: einfarbig; einfach
plainclothes *pl*	Zivilkleidung
planning officer	Beamter für Stadtplanung
pleasure	Freude
pointed	spitz
polite	höflich
to pour	*hier*: einschenken
pregnant	schwanger
pressure	Druck
to pretend	tun als ob
probable	wahrscheinlich
production facilities *pl*	Herstellungsanlagen
to punish	bestrafen
purpose	Zweck
purse	Geldbeutel
to purse one's lips	den Mund spitzen
to put sb. out of business	jmd. aus dem Markt drängen
questionable	fragwürdig

queue	Warteschlange
to race	rasen
rape	Vergewaltigung
recently	vor Kurzem
to reckon	meinen, vermuten
to reconsider	überdenken
to refuse	sich weigern
to register	sich anmelden
reluctantly	ungern, widerstrebend
remote	abgelegen
to remove	entfernen
to rephrase	umformulieren
to retire	in Ruhestand gehen
righteous	gerecht
right	Recht
rising	(an)steigend
robbery	Raubüberfall
to rock	schaukeln
row	Streit
Royal Wedding	königliche Hochzeit
to rule out	ausschließen
rumour	Gerücht
to run sb. over	jmd. überfahren
to rush off	forteilen
ϟ to sack sb.	jmd. rausschmeißen, entlassen
salad days *pl*	unschuldige Jugendjahre
salary	Gehalt
schedule	Zeitplan
scientific	wissenschaftlich
to scratch sth.	etw. kratzen
search warrant	Durchsuchungsbefehl
to sense	spüren, wahrnehmen

sensible	vernünftig
serious	ernst
to set the record straight	eine Sache richtigstellen
sexual assault	sexueller Übergriff
shadow	Schatten
shame	*hier*: Schande; Scham
shortly	gleich, in Kürze
to sigh	seufzen
sign	*hier*: Schild; Zeichen
skyscraper	Wolkenkratzer
to slam	knallen
⚡ slut	Schlampe
smartly dressed	elegant gekleidet
smitten	vernarrt
to snap at sb.	jmd. anblaffen, anschnauzen
solicitor	Rechtsanwalt
to solve sth.	etw. lösen
to speak ill of the dead	den Toten etw. Schlechtes nachsagen
speaking of which	apropos
spy	Spion(in)
to stab	erstechen
staff	Mitarbeiter, Personal
to stand down from election	von einer Wahl zurücktreten
steep	steil
steering wheel	Lenkrad
strange	seltsam, merkwürdig
successful	erfolgreich
to suffer (from)	leiden (unter)
summary	Zusammenfassung
summit	Gipfel
to sum up	zusammenfassen
(prime) suspect	(Haupt-)Verdächtige(r)

to suspect	verdächtigen
suspicious	verdächtig
suspiciously	mistrauisch
to swallow	schlucken
to swear to oneself	vor sich hin fluchten
to sweep	kehren
sympathy	Mitgefühl
to tackle	angreifen, sich stürzen auf
to take a break	Pause machen
to take a drag	einen Zug nehmen
to take a sip	einen Schluck nehmen
to take care of sb.	sich um jmd. kümmern
to take notice of sb.	jmd. beachten
to take statements	Aussagen aufnehmen
takings *pl*	Einnahmen
to tap	leicht klopfen
to tear out	ausreißen
tear	Träne
to tense	anspannen, sich verspannen
thank goodness	Gott sei Dank!
There, there!	*tröstende Worte*
ϟ to think straight	logisch/klar denken
threat	Drohung
too bad	ein Jammer
too good to be true	zu schön um wahr zu sein
traffic	Verkehr
trap	Falle
trapped	gefangen
to trust	vertrauen
trustworthy	vertrauenswürdig
to turn pale	blass werden
unarmed	unbewaffnet

unless	es sei denn
unwelcoming	nicht einladend, unwirtlich
upset	durcheinander, aufgebracht
urgent	dringend
useless	nutzlos
usually	normalerweise, gewöhnlich
valuable	wertvoll
victim	Opfer
violence	Gewalt
voice	Stimme
voice recorder	Aufzeichnungsgerät für Gespräche
wallet	*hier*: Mappe
to waste	verschwenden
wave	*hier*: ein Wink mit der Hand
wealthy	vermögend
weapon	Waffe
ϟ Whatever!	Egal!
What on earth…!	Was zum Teufel…!
to whisper	flüstern
to whistle	pfeifen
widow	Witwe
witness	Zeuge/Zeugin
witty	schlagfertig
to wonder	sich fragen

List of Exercises

Lernkrimi Lektüren Englisch

A1

A Cry in the Darkness
Kurzkrimis
ISBN 978-3-8174-9984-7

Death at Land's End
Kurzkrimis
ISBN 978-3-8174-9658-7

The Murderer Next Door
Kurzkrimis
ISBN 978-3-8174-9438-5

A2

Blood and Breakfast
Kurzkrimis
ISBN 978-3-8174-7760-9

Deadly Business
Kurzkrimis
ISBN 978-3-8174-9215-2

It Was Murder, My Lord
Kurzkrimis
ISBN 978-3-8174-7734-0

Last Exit Waterloo Bridge
Kurzkrimis
ISBN 978-3-8174-7733-3

Murder at Teatime
Kurzkrimis
ISBN 978-3-8174-7839-2

Long Time No Kill
Classic
ISBN 978-3-8174-9794-2

Murderous Collection
Sammelband 10 in 1
ISBN 978-3-8174-8967-1

B1

Bullets over Bristol
Kurzkrimis
ISBN 978-3-8174-8544-4

Death Comes Knocking
Kurzkrimis
ISBN 978-3-8174-7945-0

Murderous Network
Kurzkrimis
ISBN 978-3-8174-9312-8

Art and Ashes
Classic
ISBN 978-3-8174-9493-4

Cook and Kill
Classic
ISBN 978-3-8174-9492-7

Crime Scene Tower of London
Classic
ISBN 978-3-8174-7687-9

Deadly Mistake
Classic
ISBN 978-3-8174-8259-7

Death Wasn't the Deal
Classic
ISBN 978-3-8174-9491-0

Der Rächer von Canterbury
Classic
ISBN 978-3-8174-7662-6

Der rote Nebel
Classic
ISBN 978-3-8174-7574-2

Ein fast perfekter Coup
Classic
ISBN 978-3-8174-7568-1

The Mystery of the Mummy
Classic
ISBN 978-3-8174-7304-5

Lernkrimi Lektüren Englisch

B1

Schüsse im Nebel
Classic
ISBN 978-3-8174-7763-0

Tod eines Dandys
Classic
ISBN 978-3-8174-7660-2

Toxic Testament
Classic
ISBN 978-3-8174-7879-2

Inspector Hudson Investigates
Sammelband 3 in 1
ISBN 978-3-8174-7625-1

London Crime Time
Sammelband 3 in 1
ISBN 978-3-8174-7787-6

Bone by Bone
Lernthriller
ISBN 978-3-8174-9497-2

Massacre United
Lernthriller
ISBN 978-3-8174-9319-7

Faceless Killer
Lernthriller
ISBN 978-3-8174-8856-8

B2

Bloody Diamonds
Classic
ISBN 978-3-8174-9494-1

Das geheimnisvolle Gemälde
Classic
ISBN 978-3-8174-7306-9

Der Seelenjäger
Classic
ISBN 978-3-8174-7581-0

Der unheimliche Ritter
Classic
ISBN 978-3-8174-7661-9

Die Rache des Lords
Classic
ISBN 978-3-8174-7663-3

Die Spur des Höllenhundes
Classic
ISBN 978-3-8174-7307-6

Lady Mayfair's Revenge
Classic
ISBN 978-3-8174-7815-6

Nobody Dies Twice
Classic
ISBN 978-3-8174-9495-8

The Riddle of the Black Shoe
Classic
ISBN 978-3-8174-7638-1

Schatten der Vergangenheit
Classic
ISBN 978-3-8174-7570-4

Teuflische Intrigen
Classic
ISBN 978-3-8174-7608-4

In Terror
Lernthriller
ISBN 978-3-8174-8857-5

C1

A Scottish Murder Mystery
Classic
ISBN 978-3-8174-8379-2

Lernkrimi Hörbücher Englisch

A1

Dangerous Deals
ISBN 978-3-8174-9988-5

A2

A Shot in the Night
ISBN 978-3-8174-8202-3

Death Wish
ISBN 978-3-8174-8204-7

The Butterworth Mystery
ISBN 978-3-8174-8203-0

Strangled
ISBN 978-3-8174-9665-5

B1

Bloody Revenge
ISBN 978-3-8174-8860-5

Danger at King's Cross
ISBN 978-3-8174-7673-2

B2

Bloody Legacy
ISBN 978-3-8174-7676-3

Crime & Company
ISBN 978-3-8174-8976-3

Die Intrigantin
ISBN 978-3-8174-7675-6

Murder at the Office
ISBN 978-3-8174-7747-0

Lernkrimi Rätselblöcke Englisch

A1

Murderous Games
ISBN 978-3-8174-9500-9

A2

The Art of Crime
ISBN 978-3-8174-9155-1

B1

A Deadly Puzzle
ISBN 978-3-8174-8832-2

Lernkrimi Sprachkurs Englisch

A1/A2

Lernkrimi Sprachkurs
ISBN 978-3-8174-7844-5